W9-BUQ-557

Wishful Thinking

Other Books by Frederick Buechner

Fiction

A Long Day's Dying
The Seasons' Difference
The Return of Ansel Gibbs
The Final Beast
The Entrance to Porlock
Lion Country
Open Heart
Love Feast
Treasure Hunt
The Book of Bebb
Godric
Brendan
The Wizard's Tide
The Son of Laughter

Nonfiction

The Magnificent Defeat
The Hungering Dark
The Alphabet of Grace
The Faces of Jesus
Telling the Truth: The Gospel as Tragedy, Comedy and Fairy Tale
Peculiar Treasures: A Biblical Who's Who
The Sacred Journey
Now and Then
A Room Called Remember
Whistling in the Dark: A Doubter's Dictionary
Telling Secrets
The Clown in the Belfry

WISHFUL THINKING

A Seeker's ABC

REVISED AND EXPANDED

Frederick Buechner

HarperSanFrancisco
A Division of HarperCollins*Publishers*

A condensed version of "Bible" appeared as "The Book Almost Nobody Reads" in *The Reader's Digest,* September 1972. "Mary" and "Jesus" appeared as "Comfort for a Sorrowing Mother" and "Finality and Completion" in *The Christian Century,* March 5 and 26, 1969. Portions of "Compassion," "Mysticism," "Religion," and "Religious Books" were included in "Summons to Pilgrimage," *The New York Times Book Review,* March 16, 1969.

Library of Congress Cataloging-in-Publication Data
Buechner, Frederick, 1926–
Wishful thinking : a seeker's ABC / Frederick Buechner. — Rev. and expanded ed.
p. cm.
ISBN 0–06–061139–1 (alk. paper)
1. Theology—Dictionaries. I. Title.
BR95.B785 1993
230'.03—dc20 92–54776
CIP

01 02 RRD-H 20 19 18 17 16

For

JOHN A. KOUWENHOVEN

who gave me the idea

Contents

Author's Note

For what Wishful Thinking means, see under *W*—that is to say for what I *think* it means. Wishfully.

What follows is a kind of mongrel litter by Pascal's *Pensées,* out of Voltaire's *Dictionnaire Philosophique,* via *The Devil's Dictionary* of Ambrose Bierce. As in the case of any such enterprise, you stand to learn considerably more about the prejudices, limitations, and enthusiasms of the lexicographer than about the words in his lexicon. I suppose it can't be helped.

As for the words, most of them are so familiar or formidable or both that nobody pays much attention to them any more, and yet they stand for realities which everybody, religiously inclined or otherwise, has to keep on dealing with year after year like it or not. *Faith,* for example. One way or another, it is what gets us all out of bed in the morning. Or fails to. Needless to say, the definitions make no claim of being even close to definitive. At their best they may serve to raise an unsettled and unsettling question or two. It is in essence a Doubtful Dictionary—dubious, full of doubts, and aimed especially at doubters.

From Paul the Apostle down through C. S. Lewis, W. T. Stace, and Paul Tillich, many a better man is echoed here, and I have also pillaged shamelessly from the miscellaneous utterances of the likes of David H. C. Read, James Muilenburg, Agnes Sanford, and more. I am sure that I have unconsciously cribbed from others too. My gratitude and apologies to them all.

Aa

ABRAHAM (*See* FAITH)

ADAM AND EVE (*See* MAN)

AGNOSTIC

An agnostic is somebody who doesn't know for sure whether there really is a God. That is some people all of the time and all people some of the time.

There are some agnostics who don't know simply because they've never taken pains to try to find out—like the bear who didn't know what was on the other side of the mountain.

There are other agnostics who have taken many pains. They have climbed over the mountain, and what do you think they saw? Only the other side of the mountain. At least that was all they could be sure of. That faint glimmer on the far horizon could have been just Disneyland.

ANGELS

Sleight-of-hand magic is based on the demonstrable fact that as a rule people see only what they expect to see. Angels are powerful spirits whom God sends into the world to wish us well. Since we don't expect to see them, we don't. An angel spreads its glittering wings over us, and we say things like, "It was one of those days that made you feel good just to be alive," or "I had a hunch everything was going to turn out all right," or "I don't know where I ever found the courage."

ANGER

Of the Seven Deadly Sins, anger is possibly the most fun. To lick your wounds, to smack your lips over grievances long past, to roll over your tongue the prospect of bitter confrontations still to come, to savor to the last toothsome morsel both the pain you are given and the pain you are giving back—in many ways it is a feast fit for a king. The chief drawback is that what you are wolfing down is yourself. The skeleton at the feast is you.

ANNUNCIATION

Mary couldn't say she wasn't warned. The angel came with an Easter lily in his hand and stood so still he could have been one of the columns in the loggia where they met. Mary had trouble hearing what he said and afterward thought it might have been just a dream. Even so it troubled her.

It was not until later that the real trouble came. The real trouble came when what the angel announced would happen happened, but in a way she couldn't have dreamed: squatting there in the straw with her thighs wrenched apart, while out of her pain she dropped into the howling world something that looked like nothing so much as raw beefsteak: who was the one the angel had said was to be called Holy, the Son of the Most High: who was the Word itself fleshed with—of all flesh—hers.

ATHEIST

A true atheist is one who is willing to face the full consequences of what it means to say there is no God.

To say there is no God means among other things that there are no Absolute Standards. For instance, an atheist may believe with all his heart that murder is wrong, but if he runs into somebody else who believes with all his heart that murder isn't wrong as long as you can get away with it, there is no Absolute Standard by which it can be shown that one view is better than the other, just as there is no Absolute Standard by which it can be shown that vanilla is better than chocolate.

If an atheist says that murder is wrong because it works against the good of society in general then he is saying that the good of society in general is gooder than the good of the murderer in particular, and having thrown out all Absolute Standards, he can't say that. All he can say is that vanilla is better than chocolate because he likes it better and so do most of his friends.

If he says, "In the absence of Absolute Standards, I declare that murder is wrong in the name of *common sense,*" then he has simply made common sense his Absolute Standard. What is in accord with common sense is Right and what isn't is Wrong.

What is American is Right and what is un-American is Wrong. What is ethical is Right and what is unethical is Wrong. What works is Right and what doesn't work is Wrong. These all bring God back under different names: Nationalism, Ethics, Pragmatism. To be a true atheist is to acknowledge no rule except the rule of thumb (*see* IDOLATRY).

Thus many an atheist is a believer without knowing it, just as many a believer is an atheist without knowing it. You can sincerely believe there is no God and live as though there is. You can sincerely believe there is a God and live as though there isn't. So it goes.

Lots of the time atheism isn't bad fun. I do what seems right to me and you do what seems right to you, and if we come into conflict with each other, society has human judges to invoke human laws and arbitrate between us. Who needs a Divine Judge and a Cosmic Law? We can learn to live in lower case.

Except sometimes. Sometimes it's almost as hard to believe God doesn't exist as to believe he does. I don't mean a baby's smile, which is probably gas. I don't mean the beauty of nature, which is always soon followed by the indifferent cruelty and ugliness of nature. I mean an atheist is about as likely as anybody else to walk into a newsstand someday and pick up a copy of the *National Enquirer* or some such paper. On the front page is a picture of a dead child. The bare back is covered with welts. The eyes are swollen shut. Both arms are broken. The full story is on page three if you have the stomach for it.

To be consistent with his creed, an atheist can say no more than that to beat a child to death is wrong with a small *w*. Wrong because it is cruel, ugly, inhuman, pointless, illegal, and makes the gorge rise. But what is apt to rise along with the gorge is the suspicion that it is wrong also with a capital *W*—the suspicion that the law that has been broken here is not just a human law, but a law as immutable as the law of gravity, one by which even if there were no children in the universe and no grown-ups to beat them, it would be written into the very fabric of reality itself that such an act is wrong.

The atheist holds the tabloid in his hand and asks the question, Why should such things happen? Atheism can reply only, Why *shouldn't* such things happen? But he keeps on asking.

What makes it hard to be an atheist is the feeling you sometimes get in the pit of your stomach that there must be after all, mad as it seems, an absolute good in terms of which such an act as this can be denounced as absolutely evil. Thus the problem of good is a major stumbling block for atheism just as the problem of evil (q.v.) is a major stumbling block for religious faith. Both must learn how to live with their doubts.

A true atheist takes human freedom very seriously. With no God to point the way, humans must find their own way. With no God to save the world, humans must save their own world if it's going to be saved. They must save it from themselves if nothing else. A true atheist does no dance on the grave of God.

The laughter of faith in God is like Abraham's laughter when God says his ninety-year-old wife is in a family way (*see* FAITH). The laughter of faith in no-God is heard in Sartre's story "The Wall": A man is threatened with death if he doesn't betray the whereabouts of his friend to the enemy. The man refuses to do this and sends the enemy on a wild goose chase to a place where he knows his friend isn't. By chance it turns out to be the very place where his friend is. The friend is captured and executed and the man given his freedom. Sartre ends the story by saying that the man laughed till he cried.

AVARICE

Avarice, greed, concupiscence, and so forth are all based on the mathematical truism that the more you get, the more you have. The remark of Jesus that it is more blessed to give than to receive (Acts 20:35) is based on the human truth that the more you give away in love, the more you are. It is not just for the sake of other people that Jesus tells us to give rather than get, but for our own sakes too.

Bb

BAPTISM

Baptism consists of getting dunked or sprinkled. Which technique is used matters about as much as whether you pray kneeling or standing on your head. Dunking is a better symbol, however. Going under symbolizes the end of everything about your life that is less than human. Coming up again symbolizes the beginning in you of something strange and new and hopeful. You can breathe again.

Question: How about infant baptism? Shouldn't you wait until the child grows up enough to know what's going on?

Answer: If you don't think there is as much of the less-than-human in an infant as there is in anybody else, you have lost touch with reality.

When it comes to the forgiving and transforming love of God, one wonders if the six-week-old screecher knows all that much less than the Archbishop of Canterbury about what's going on.

BIBLE

There are people who say we should read the Bible as literature. The advice has a pleasantly modern and reasonable ring to it. We are all attracted. Read the Bible for the story it tells. Read the King James Version especially for the power of its prose and the splendor of its poetry. Read it for the history it contains and for its insights into ancient ways. Don't worry about whatever it's supposed to mean to religious faith. Don't bother about the hocus-pocus. Read it like any other book.

The trouble is it's not like any other book. To read the Bible as literature is like reading *Moby Dick* as a whaling manual or *The Brothers Karamazov* for its punctuation.

Like *The Divine Comedy, Don Quixote, Paradise Lost,* or Proust, the Bible hangs heavy on many a conscience. One ought to have read it—if not for religious reasons, then simply because it has left so deep a mark on Western civilization. One usually hasn't. Some parts of Genesis maybe, a handful of Psalms, a sampling or two from the Gospels. And that's about it.

There are good reasons for not reading it. Its format is almost supernaturally forbidding: the binding rusty black like an undertaker's cutaway, the double columns of a timetable, the print of a phone book, cluttered margins, and a text so overloaded with guides to pronunciation ("Jē'-ṣŭs came from Năz'-ă-rĕth of Găl'-i-lēe and was baptized of Jŏhn in Jôr'-dăn") and so befouled with inexplicable italics ("Nō'-ăh only remained *alive,* and they that *were* with him in the ark") that reading it is like listening to somebody with a bad stutter. More often than not the poetry is printed as prose, and poetry and prose alike are chopped up into entirely arbitrary chapters and verses, so that one of the major poems in the Old Testament, for instance, begins toward the end of Isaiah 52 with (in some versions) nothing to suggest that Isaiah 53 is a continuation of it or that it is a poem at all.

There are other reasons for not reading the Bible. It not only looks awfully dull, but some of it is. The prophets are wildly repetitious and almost never know when to stop. There are all the *begats.* There are passages that even Moses must have nodded over, like the six long chapters in Exodus (25–30) that describe the tabernacle and its workings all the way from the length, breadth, and composition of the curtains down to the color and cut of the priest's ephod and a recipe for anointing oil. There are the lists of kings, dietary laws, tribes, and tribal territories. There is the Book of Leviticus and most of the Book of Numbers. There are places where the parallelism of Hebrew poetry ("Pour out thy indignation upon them / and let thy burning anger overtake them. May their camp be a desolation, / let no one dwell in their tents") becomes irresistibly soporific. There is the sense you have that you know what the Bible is going to say before it says it. There are all those familiar quotations. There is the phrase "the Good Book." Give me a bad book any day.

There are still more reasons. The barbarities, for instance. The often fanatical nationalism. The passages where the God of Israel is depicted as interested in other nations only to the degree that he can use them to whip Israel into line. God hardening Pharaoh's heart and then clobbering him for hard-heartedness. The self-righteousness and self-pity of many of the Psalms, plus their frequent vindictiveness. The way the sublime and the unspeakable are always jostling each other. The 137th Psalm, for example, which starts out "By the waters of Babylon, there we sat down and wept" and ends "Happy shall he be who takes your little ones and dashes them against the rock!" Or Noah, the one man left worth saving, God's blue-eyed old sailorman, getting drunk in port and passing out in a tent where his son Ham beholds his shame. Or the Book of Deuteronomy, where there are laws thousands of years ahead of their time, like the one that says a newly married man is exempt from military service for a year so "he can be happy with the wife whom he has taken," side by side with laws that would make Genghis Khan blush, like the one that says Israel is to destroy conquered peoples utterly, making no covenants with them and showing no mercy. Or even Jesus of Nazareth, the same Jesus who in one place uses a Samaritan of all people—a member of a hated tribe—as the example of a man who truly loves his neighbor, and in another place is quoted as telling a Canaanite woman who came to him for help that it was not fair for him to throw the children's food to the dogs.

In short, one way to describe the Bible, written by many different people over a period of three thousand years and more, would be to say that it is a disorderly collection of sixty-odd books which are often tedious, barbaric, obscure, and teem with contradictions and inconsistencies. It is a swarming compost of a book, an Irish stew of poetry and propaganda, law and legalism, myth and murk, history and hysteria. Over the centuries it has become hopelessly associated with tub-thumping evangelism and dreary piety, with superannuated superstition and blue-nosed moralizing, with ecclesiastical authoritarianism and crippling literalism. Let them who try to start out at Genesis and work their way conscientiously to Revelation beware.

And yet—

And yet just because it is a book about both the sublime and the unspeakable, it is a book also about life the way it really is. It is a book about people who at one and the same time can be both believing and unbelieving, innocent and guilty, crusaders and crooks, full of hope and full of despair. In other words, it is a book about us.

And it is also a book about God. If it is not about the God we believe in, then it is about the God we do not believe in. One way or another, the story we find in the Bible is our own story.

But we find something else in it too. The great Protestant theologian Karl Barth says that reading the Bible is like looking out of the window and seeing everybody on the street shading their eyes with their hands and gazing up into the sky toward something which is hidden from us by the roof. They are pointing up. They are speaking strange words. They are very excited. Something is happening which we can't see happening. Or something is about to happen.

Something beyond our comprehension has caught them up and is seeking to lead them on "from land to land for strange, intense, uncertain, and yet mysteriously well-planned service."[1]

To read the Bible is to try to read the expression on their faces. To listen to the words of the Bible is to try to catch the sound of the queer, dangerous, and compelling word they seem to hear.

Abraham and Sarah with tears of incredulous laughter running down their ancient cheeks when God tells them that he is going to keep his promise and give them the son they have always wanted. King David, all but naked as the day he was born, dancing for joy in front of the ark. Paul struck dumb on the road to Damascus. Jesus of Nazareth stretched out between two crooks, with dried Roman spit on his face. They are all of them looking up. And listening.

How do twentieth-century men and women, with all their hang-ups, try to see what they were looking at and hear what it was they heard? What follows are some practical suggestions on how to read the Bible without tears. Or maybe with them.

1. Don't start at the beginning and try to plow your way straight through to the end. At least not without help. If you do, you're almost sure to bog down somewhere around the twenty-fifth chapter of Exodus. Concentrate on the high points at first. There is much to reward you in the valleys too, but at the outset keep to the upper elevations. There are quite a few.

There is the vivid eyewitness account of the reign of King David, for instance (2 Samuel plus the first two chapters of 1 Kings), especially the remarkable chapters that deal with his last years, when the crimes and blunders of his youth have

1. Karl Barth, *The Word of God and the Word of Men* (New York: Harper Torchbooks, 1957), 63.

begun to catch up with him. Or the Joseph stories (Genesis 39–50). Or the Book of Job. Or the Sermon on the Mount (Matthew 5–7). Or the seventh chapter of Paul's letter to the Romans, which states as lucidly as it has ever been stated the basic moral dilemma of humankind, and then leads into the eighth chapter, which contains the classic expression of Christianity's basic hope.

2. The air in such upper altitudes is apt to be clearer and brighter than elsewhere; but if you nevertheless find yourself getting lost along the way, try a good Bible commentary which gives the date and historical background of each book, explains the special circumstances which it was written to meet, and verse by verse tries to illumine the meaning of the difficult sections. Even when the meaning seems perfectly clear, a commentary can greatly enrich your understanding. The Book of Jonah, for instance—only two or three pages long and the one genuine comedy in the Old Testament—takes on added significance when you discover its importance in advancing the idea that God's love is extended not just to the children of Israel, but to all humankind.

3. If you have even as much as a nodding acquaintance with a foreign language, try reading the Bible in that. Then you stand a chance of hearing what the Bible is actually saying instead of what you assume it must be saying because it is the Bible. Some of it you may hear in such a new way that it is as if you had never heard it before. "Blessed are the meek" is the way the English version goes, whereas in French it comes out, "*Heureux sont les débonnaires*" (Happy are the debonair). The *debonair* of all things! Doors fly open. Bells ring out.

4. If you don't know a foreign language, try some English version that you've never tried before—Today's English Version, Goodspeed's translation, J. B. Phillips' New Testament, or any other you can lay your hands on. The more far-out the better. Nothing could be farther out than the Bible itself. The

trouble with the King James or Authorized Version is that it is too full of Familiar Quotations. The trouble with Familiar Quotations is that they are so familiar you don't hear them. When Jesus was crucified, the Romans nailed over his head a sign saying "King of the Jews" so nobody would miss the joke. To get something closer to the true flavor, try translating the sign instead: "Head Jew."

5. It may sound like fortune-telling, but don't let that worry you: Let the Bible fall open in your lap and start there. If you don't find something that speaks to you, let it fall open to something else. Read it as though it were as exotic as the *I Ching* or the Tarot deck. Because it is.

6. If people claim that you have to take the Bible literally, word for word, or not at all, ask them if you have to take John the Baptist literally when he calls Jesus the Lamb of God.

If people claim that no rational person can take a book seriously that assumes the world was created in six days and man in an afternoon, ask them if they can take Shakespeare seriously, whose scientific knowledge would have sent a third-grader into peals of laughter.

7. Finally this. If you look *at* a window, you see flyspecks, dust, the crack where Junior's Frisbee hit it. If you look *through* a window, you see the world beyond.

Something like this is the difference between those who see the Bible as a Holy Bore and those who see it as the Word of God, which speaks out of the depths of an almost unimaginable past into the depths of ourselves.

BLESSING

The word "blessing" has come to mean more often than not a pious formality such as ministers are continually being roped into giving at high school graduations, Rotarian wienie roasts and the like, and to say "God bless you" to a person, unless that person happens to have just sneezed, is generally regarded as a pious eccentricity. It was not always so.

In the biblical sense, if you give me your blessing, you irreversibly convey into my life not just something of the beneficent power and vitality of who you are but something also of the life-giving power of God in whose name the blessing is given. Even after old, half-blind Isaac discovered that he had been hoodwinked into blessing the wrong twin, he could no more take the blessing back and give it to Esau again than he could take the words of it out of the air and put them back into his mouth again.

Religious language has come to such a pass that perhaps "luck," of all words, suggests the reality of this better than "blessing." Everybody knows that luck has magic in it and that when you have it, you really have something. It may see you through hard times. It may win you the sweepstakes. A blessing, on the other hand, has come to seem something on the order of a Hallmark friendship card.

BODY (*See* IMMORTALITY, SEX)

BREAD

Man does not live by bread alone, but he also does not live long without it. To eat is to acknowledge our dependence—both on food and on each other. It also reminds us of other kinds of emptiness that not even the Blue Plate Special can touch. (*See also* GLUTTONY.)

BUDDHISM (*See* REVELATION, TOLERATION)

BUECHNER

It is my name. It is pronounced Beekner. If somebody mispronounces it in some foolish way, I have the feeling that what's foolish is me. If somebody forgets it, I feel that it's I who am forgotten. There's something about it that embarrasses me in just the same way that there's something about me that embarrasses me. I can't imagine myself with any other name—Held, say, or Merrill, or Hlavacek. If my name were different, I would be different. When I tell you my name, I have given you a hold over me that you didn't have before. If you call it out, I stop, look, and listen whether I want to or not.

In the Book of Exodus, God tells Moses that his name is Yahweh, and God hasn't had a peaceful moment since.

Cc

CHARITY (*See* LOVE, SIN)

CHASTITY

Mark Twain speaks somewhere of "a good man in the worst sense of the word." A chaste person in the worst sense of the word is one whose chastity is fear and prudery masquerading as moral one-upmanship. A chaste person in the best sense of the word is somebody on the order of a priest who gives up sex in general and marriage in particular so that the Church can be his better half and the whole parish his children.

CHILDREN

When the disciples, overearnest as ever, asked Jesus who was the greatest in the kingdom of Heaven, Jesus pulled a child out of the crowd and said the greatest in the kingdom of Heaven were people like this (Matthew 18:1–4). Two thousand years of homiletic sentimentalizing to the contrary notwithstanding, Jesus was not playing Captain Kangaroo. He was saying that the people who get into Heaven are people who, like children, don't worry about it too much. They are people who, like children, live with their hands open more than with their fists clenched. They are people who, like children, are so relatively unburdened by preconceptions that if somebody says there's a pot of gold at the end of the rainbow, they are perfectly willing to go take a look for themselves.

Children aren't necessarily better than other people. Like the child in "The Emperor's New Clothes," they are just apt to be better at telling the difference between a put-up job and the real thing.

CHRIST (*See* MESSIAH, JESUS, CROSS, ISRAEL, GOSPEL)

CHRISTIAN

Some think of a Christian as one who necessarily *believes* certain things. That Jesus was the son of God, say. Or that Mary was a virgin. Or that the Pope is infallible. Or that all other religions are all wrong.

Some think of a Christian as one who necessarily *does* certain things. Such as going to church. Getting baptized. Giving up liquor and tobacco. Reading the Bible. Doing a good deed a day.

Some think of a Christian as just a Nice Guy.

Jesus said, "I am the way, and the truth, and the life; no one comes to the Father, but by me" (John 14:6). He didn't say that any particular ethic, doctrine, or religion was the way, the truth, and the life. He said that he was. He didn't say that it was by believing or doing anything in particular that you could "come to the Father." He said that it was only by him—by living, participating in, being caught up by the way of life that he embodied, that was his way.

Thus it is possible to be on Christ's way and with his mark upon you without ever having heard of Christ, and for that reason to be on your way to God though maybe you don't even believe in God.

A Christian is one who is on the way, though not necessarily very far along it, and who has at least some dim and half-baked idea of whom to thank.

A Christian isn't necessarily any nicer than anybody else. Just better informed.

CHURCH

The visible church is all the people who get together from time to time in God's name. Anybody can find out who they are by going to church to look.

The invisible church is all the people God uses for his hands and feet in this world. Nobody can find out who they are except God.

Think of them as two circles. The optimist says they are concentric. The cynic says they don't even touch. The realist says they occasionally overlap.

In a fit of high inspiration, the author of the Book of Revelation states that there is no temple in the New Jerusalem, thus squelching once and for all the tedious quip that since Heaven is an endless church service, anybody with two wits to rub together would prefer Hell.

The reason for there being no temple in the New Jerusalem is presumably the same as the reason for Noah's leaving the ark behind when he finally makes it to Mount Ararat.

COINCIDENCE

I think of a person I haven't seen or thought of for years, and ten minutes later I see her crossing the street. I turn on the radio to hear a voice reading the biblical story of Jael, which is the story that I have spent the morning writing about. A car passes me on the road, and its license plate consists of my wife's and my initials side by side. When you tell people stories like that, their usual reaction is to laugh. One wonders why.

I believe that people laugh at coincidence as a way of relegating it to the realm of the absurd and of therefore not having to take seriously the possibility that there is a lot more going on in our lives than we either know or care to know. Who can say what it is that's going on, but I suspect that part of it, anyway, is that every once and so often we hear a whisper from the wings that goes something like this: "You've turned up in the right place at the right time. You're doing fine. Don't ever think that you've been forgotten."

COMPASSION

Compassion is the sometimes fatal capacity for feeling what it's like to live inside somebody else's skin.

It is the knowledge that there can never really be any peace and joy for me until there is peace and joy finally for you too.

CONFESSION

To confess your sins to God is not to tell him anything he doesn't already know. Until you confess them, however, they are the abyss between you. When you confess them, they become the Golden Gate bridge.

CONVERSION (*See* REPENTANCE)

COVENANT

Old Testament means Old Covenant means the old agreement that was arrived at between God and Israel at Mount Sinai with Moses presiding. "I shall be your God and you shall be my people" (Leviticus 26:12) sums it up—i.e., if you obey God's commandments, God will love you.

New Testament means New Covenant means the new agreement that was arrived at by God alone in an upstairs room in Jerusalem with Jesus presiding. Jesus sums it up by raising his wine and saying, "This cup is the new covenant in my blood" (1 Corinthians 11:25).

Like Moses, Jesus believed that if you obey God, God will love you, but here he is saying something beyond that. He is saying if you don't obey God, that doesn't mean that God won't love you. It means simply that God's love becomes a suffering love: a love that suffers because it is not reciprocated, a love that suffers because we who are loved suffer and suffer precisely *in* our failure to reciprocate. By giving us the cup to drink, Jesus is saying that in loving us God "bleeds" for us—not "even though" we don't give a damn, but precisely *because* we don't. God keeps his part of the covenant whether we keep our part or not; it's just that one way costs him more.

This idea that God loves people whether or not they give a damn isn't new. In the Old Testament Book of Hosea, for instance, the prophet portrays God as lashing out at Israel for their disobedience and saying that by all rights they should be wiped off the face of the earth, but then adding, "How can I hand you over, O Israel? . . . My heart recoils within me. . . . I will not execute my fierce anger . . . for I am God and not man, the Holy One in your midst, and I will not come to destroy" (Hosea 11:8–9).

What *is* new about the New Covenant, therefore, is not the idea that God loves the world enough to bleed for it but the claim that here he is actually putting his money where his mouth is. Like a father saying about his sick child, "I'd do anything to make you well," God finally calls his own bluff and does it. Jesus Christ is what God does, and the cross where he did it is the central symbol of New Covenant faith.

So what? *Does* the suffering of the father for the sick child make the sick child well? In the last analysis, we each have to answer for ourselves.

Like the elderly Christ Church don who was heard muttering over his chop at high table, "This mutton is as hard to swallow as the Lamb of God," there are some who find the whole idea simply unswallowable—just the idea of *God,* let alone the idea of God in Christ submitting to the cross for love's sake. Yet down through the centuries there have been others—good ones and bad ones, bright ones and stupid ones—who with varying degrees of difficulty have been able to swallow it and have claimed that what they swallowed made the difference between life and death (*see* LORD'S SUPPER).

Such people would also tend to claim that whereas to respond to the Old Covenant is to become righteous, to respond to the New Covenant is to become new. The proof, they might add, is in the pudding.

CREATION

To *make* suggests making something out of something else the way a carpenter makes wooden boxes out of wood. To *create* suggests making something out of nothing the way an artist makes paintings or poems. It is true that artists, like carpenters, have to use something else—paint, words—but the beauty or meaning they make is different from the material they make it out of. To create is to make something essentially new.

When God created the Creation, he made something where before there had been nothing, and as the author of the Book of Job puts it, "the morning stars sang together, and all the sons of God shouted for joy" (Job 38:7) at the sheer and shimmering novelty of the thing. "New every morning is the love / Our wakening and uprising prove" says the hymn. Using the same old materials of earth, air, fire, and water, every twenty-four hours God creates something new out of them. If you think you're seeing the same show all over again seven times a week, you're crazy. Every morning you wake up to something that in all eternity never was before and never will be again. And the you that wakes up was never the same before and will never be the same again either.

CROSS

Two of the noblest pillars of the ancient world—Roman law and Jewish piety—together supported the necessity of putting Jesus Christ to death in a manner that even for its day was peculiarly loathsome. Thus the cross stands for the tragic folly of human beings, not just at their worst but at their best.

Jesus needn't have died. Presumably he could have followed the advice of friends like Peter and avoided the showdown. Instead he chose to die because he believed that he had to if the world was to be saved. Thus the cross stands for the best that human beings can do as well as for the worst.

"My God, my God, why hast thou forsaken me?" Jesus died in the profoundest sense alone. Thus the cross stands for the inevitable dereliction and defeat of the best and the worst indiscriminately.

For those who believe that Jesus Christ rose from the dead early on a Sunday morning, and for those also who believe that he provided food for worms just as the rest of us will, the conclusion is inescapable that he came out somehow the winner. What emerged from his death was a kind of way, of truth, of life, without which the last two thousand years of human history would be even more tragic than they are.

A six-pointed star, a crescent moon, a lotus—the symbols of other religions suggest beauty and light. The symbol of Christianity is an instrument of death. It suggests, at the very least, hope.

Dd

DEATH (*See* LIFE, IMMORTALITY, PURGATORY, LAW)

DESPAIR

Despair has been called the unforgivable sin—not presumably because God refuses to forgive it but because it despairs of the possibility of being forgiven.

DEVIL

To take the Devil seriously is to take seriously the fact that the total evil in the world is greater than the sum of all its parts. Likewise the total evil in yourself. The murderer who says, "I couldn't help it" isn't necessarily just kidding.

To take the Devil seriously is also to take seriously our total and spine-tingling freedom. Lucifer was an angel who even in Paradise itself was free to get the Hell out.

DISCIPLE (*See* MINISTER)

DIVINITY OF CHRIST (*See* WORD)

DOCTRINE

No matter how fancy and metaphysical a doctrine sounds, it was a human experience first. The doctrine of the divinity of Christ, for instance. The place it began was not the word processor of some fourth-century Greek theologian but the experience of basically untheological people who had known

Jesus of Nazareth and found something happening to their lives which had never happened before.

Unless you can somehow participate yourself in the experience that lies behind a doctrine, simply to subscribe to it doesn't mean much. Sometimes, however, simply to subscribe to a doctrine is the first step toward experiencing the reality that lies behind it.

DOUBT

Whether your faith is that there is a God or that there is not a God, if you don't have any doubts, you are either kidding yourself or asleep. Doubts are the ants in the pants of faith. They keep it awake and moving.

There are two principal kinds of doubt, one of the head and the other of the stomach.

In my head there is almost nothing I can't doubt when the fit is upon me—the divinity of Christ, the efficacy of the sacraments, the significance of the Church, the existence of God. But even when I am at my most skeptical, I go on with my life as though nothing untoward has happened.

I have never experienced stomach doubt, but I think Jesus did. When he cried out, "My God, my God, why hast thou forsaken me!" I don't think he was raising a theological issue any more than he was quoting the Twenty-second Psalm. I think he had looked into the abyss itself and found there a darkness that spiritually, viscerally, totally engulfed him. I think God allows that kind of darkness to happen only to his saints. The rest of us aren't up to doubting that way—or maybe believing that way either.

When our faith is strongest, we believe with our hearts as well as with our heads, but only at a few rare moments, I think, do we feel in our stomachs what it must be like to be engulfed by light.

Ee

ELECTION (*See* ISRAEL)

ENVIRONMENT

It's too bad that such a poor word has come to refer to something so rich. The forests, the rivers, the mountains, the oceans, the deserts, the beaches, the fields, the flowers, the rain, the sky, the air. To speak of them collectively as the *environment* is to suggest that they are somehow antiseptic, impersonal, lifeless. It makes it almost possible to forget that what we are in danger of ruining through our rapacity and folly is the mother who bore us and the green grave that awaits us. Is our hearts' delight. Is home.

ENVY

Envy is the consuming desire to have everybody else as unsuccessful as you are.

ESCAPISM

Religion has often been denounced as escapism, and it often is. To deny the prevalence of pain in the world and the perennial popularity of evil. To abdicate responsibility for them by assuming that God will take care of them very nicely on his own. To accept them as divine judgment upon the sins especially of other people. To dismiss them or to encourage others to dismiss them by stressing the promise of pie in the sky. To pretend like a Forest Lawn cosmetologist that there's no such thing as death. To maintain your faith by refusing to face any nasty fact that threatens it. These are all ways of escaping reality through religion and should be denounced right along with such other modes of escape as liquor, drugs, TV, or any simplistic optimism such as Communism, anti-Communism, jingoism, right-wing evangelicalism, moralism, idealism, and so on, which assume that if everybody would only see it our way, evil would vanish and all would be sweetness and light.

But the desire to escape is not always something to be denounced, as any prisoner or slave could tell you. Jesus said, "If you continue in my word, you are truly my disciples, and you will know the truth, and the truth will make you free" (John 8:31–32). Free from sin, he explained when they pressed him. Free from imprisonment within the narrow walls of your own not-all-that-enlightened self-interest. Free from enslavement to your own shabbiest instincts, deceits, and self-deceptions. Freedom not *from* responsibility but *for* it. Escape not from reality but into it.

The best moments we any of us have as human beings are those moments when for a little while it is possible to escape the squirrel-cage of being *me* into the landscape of being *us*.

ETERNAL LIFE

When you are with somebody you love, you have little if any sense of the passage of time, and you also have, in the fullest sense of the phrase, a *good* time.

When you are with God, you have something like the same experience. The biblical term for the experience is Eternal Life. Another is Heaven.

What does it mean to be "with God"? It doesn't mean you have to be thinking about being with God, or feeling religious, or sitting in church, or saying your prayers, though it might mean any or all of these. It doesn't even mean you have to believe in God.

To say that a person is "with it" is slang for saying that whether he's playing an electric guitar or just watching the clouds roll by, he's so caught up in what he's doing and so totally himself while he's doing it that there's none of him left over to be doing anything else with in the back of his head or out of the corner of his eye. It's slang for saying that the temperature where she is is about forty degrees hotter than the temperature where she is not, and that whatever it is everybody's looking for, she's found it, and that if she were a flag and they ran her up the mast, we'd all have to salute whether we liked it or not. And the chances are we'd like it.

If the It you're with when you're really "with it" isn't God, it's enough like him to be his brother.

We think of Eternal Life, if we think of it at all, as what happens when life ends. We would do better to think of it as what happens when life begins.

Saint Paul uses the phrase Eternal Life to describe the end and goal of the process of salvation (q.v.). Elsewhere he writes the same thing in a remarkable sentence in which he says that the whole purpose of God's slogging around through the muck of history and of our own individual histories is somehow to prod us, jolly us, worry us, cajole us, and if need be, bludgeon us into reaching "mature manhood . . . the measure of the stature of the fullness of Christ" (Ephesians 4:13).

In other words, to live Eternal Life in the full and final sense is to be with God as Christ is with him, and with each other as Christ is with us.

ETERNITY

Eternity is not endless time or the opposite of time. It is the essence of time.

If you spin a pinwheel fast enough, then all its colors blend into a single color—white—which is the essence of all the colors of the spectrum combined.

If you spin time fast enough, then time-past, time-present, and time-to-come all blend into a single timelessness or eternity, which is the essence of all times combined.

As human beings we know time as a passing of unrepeatable events in the course of which everything passes away—including ourselves. As human beings, we also know occasions when we stand outside the passing of events and glimpse their meaning. Sometimes an event occurs in our lives (a birth, a death, a marriage—some event of unusual beauty, pain, joy) through which we catch a glimpse of what our lives are all about and maybe even what life itself is all about, and this glimpse of what "it's all about" involves not just the present but the past and future too.

Inhabitants of time that we are, we stand on such occasions with one foot in eternity. God, as Isaiah says (57:15), "inhabiteth eternity" but stands with one foot in time. The part of time where he stands most particularly is Christ, and thus in Christ we catch a glimpse of what eternity is all about, what God is all about, and what we ourselves are all about too.

EUCHARIST (*See* LORD'S SUPPER)

EVIL

- God is all-powerful.
- God is all-good.
- Terrible things happen.

You can reconcile any two of these propositions with each other, but you can't reconcile all three. The problem of evil is perhaps the greatest single problem for religious faith.

There have been numerous theological and philosophical attempts to solve it, but when it comes down to the reality of evil itself, they are none of them worth much. When a child is raped and murdered, the parents are not apt to take much comfort from the explanation (better than most) that since

God wants us to love him, we must be free to love or not to love and thus free to rape and murder a child if we take a notion to.

Christian Science solves the problem of evil by saying that it does not exist except as an illusion of mortal mind. Buddhism solves it in terms of reincarnation and an inexorable law of cause and effect whereby the raped child is merely reaping the consequences of evil deeds it committed in another life.

Christianity, on the other hand, ultimately offers no theoretical solution at all. It merely points to the cross and says that, practically speaking, there is no evil so dark and so obscene—not even this—but that God can turn it to good. (*See also* ATHEIST, JOB.)

Ff

FAITH

When God told Abraham, who was a hundred at the time, that at the age of ninety his wife Sarah was finally going to have a baby, Abraham came close to knocking himself out—"fell on his face and laughed," as Genesis puts it (17:17). In another version of the story (18:8 ff.), Sarah is hiding behind the door eavesdropping, and here it's Sarah herself who nearly splits a gut—although when God asks her about it afterward, she denies it. "No, but you did laugh," God says, thus having the last word as well as the first. God doesn't seem to hold their outbursts against them, however. On the contrary, he tells them the baby's going to be a boy and that he wants them to name him Isaac. Isaac in Hebrew means *laughter.*

Why did the two old crocks laugh? They laughed because they knew only a fool would believe that a woman with one foot in the grave was soon going to have her other foot in the maternity ward. They laughed because God expected them to believe it anyway. They laughed because God seemed to believe it. They laughed because they half-believed it themselves. They laughed because laughing felt better than crying. They laughed because if by some crazy chance it just happened to come true, they would really have something to laugh about, and in the meanwhile it helped keep them going.

Faith is "the assurance of things hoped for, the conviction of things not seen," says the Epistle to the Hebrews (11:1). Faith is laughter at the promise of a child called laughter.

If someone had come up to Jesus when he was on the cross and asked him if it hurt, he might have answered, like the man in the old joke, "Only when I laugh." But he wouldn't have been joking. Faith dies, as it lives, laughing.

Faith is better understood as a verb than as a noun, as a process than as a possession. It is on-again-off-again rather than once-and-for-all. Faith is not being sure where you're going, but going anyway. A journey without maps. Tillich said that doubt isn't the opposite of faith; it is an element of faith.

I have faith that my friend is my friend. It is possible that all his motives are ulterior. It is possible that what he is secretly drawn to is not me but my wife or my money. But there's something about the way I feel when he's around, about the way he looks me in the eye, about the way we can talk to each other without pretense and be silent together without embarrassment, that makes me willing to put my life in his hands as I do each time I call him friend.

I can't prove the friendship of my friend. When I experience it, I don't need to prove it. When I don't experience it, no proof will do. If I tried to put his friendship to the test somehow, the test itself would queer the friendship I was testing. So it is with the Godness of God.

The five so-called proofs for the existence of God will never prove to unfaith that God exists (*see* GOD). They are merely five ways of describing the existence of the God you have faith in already.

Almost nothing that makes any real difference can be proved. I can prove the law of gravity by dropping a shoe out the window. I can prove that the world is round if I'm clever at that sort of thing—that the radio works, that light travels faster than sound. I cannot prove that life is better than death or love better than hate. I cannot prove the greatness of the great or the beauty of the beautiful. I cannot even prove my own free will; maybe my most heroic act, my truest love, my deepest thought, are all just subtler versions of what happens when the doctor taps my knee with his little rubber hammer and my foot jumps.

Faith can't prove a damned thing. Or a blessed thing either.

FEET

"How beautiful upon the mountains are the feet of him who brings good tidings," says Isaiah (52:7). Not how beautiful are the herald's *lips* which proclaim the good tidings, or his *eyes* as he proclaims them, or even the good tidings themselves, but how beautiful are the *feet*—the feet without which he could never have made it up into the mountains, without which the good tidings would never have been proclaimed at all.

Who knows in what inspired way the heart, mind, spirit of the herald came to receive the good tidings of peace and salvation in the first place, but as to the question whether he would actually do something about them—put his money where his mouth was, his shoe leather where his inspiration was—his feet were the ones that finally had to decide. Maybe it is always so.

When the disciples first came upon the risen Christ that Sunday morning of their confusion and terror, it wasn't his healing hands they touched or his teaching lips or his holy heart. Instead it was those same ruined, tired dogs that had carried him to them three years earlier, when they were at their accounts and their nets, that had dragged him all the way from Galilee to Jerusalem, that had stumbled up the hill where what was to happen happened. "They took hold of his *feet* and worshiped him," Matthew says (28:9; italics mine).

Generally speaking, if you want to know who you really are, as distinct from who you like to think you are, keep an eye on where your feet take you.

FOOL

Worldly wisdom is what more or less all of us have been living by since the Stone Age. It is best exemplified by such homely utterances as *You've got your own life to lead, Business is business, Charity begins at home, Don't get involved, God helps those who help themselves, Safety first,* and so forth.

Although this wisdom can lead on occasion to ruthlessness and indifference, it is by no means incompatible with Niceness, as the life of anyone apt to read (or write) a book like this bears witness. We can be basically interested in nothing so much as feathering our own nests and still give generously to the American Cancer Society, be on the Board of Deacons, run for town office, and have a soft spot in our hearts for children and animals.

It is in contrast to all this that what Saint Paul calls "the foolishness of God" looks so foolish. Inspection stickers used to have printed on the back "Drive carefully—the life you save may be your own." That is worldly wisdom in a nutshell. What God says, on the other hand, is "The life you save is the life you lose." In other words, the life you clutch, hoard, guard, and play safe with is in the end a life worth little to anybody, including yourself, and only a life given away for love's sake is a life worth living. To bring his point home, God shows us a man who gave his life away to the extent of dying a national disgrace without a penny in the bank or a friend to his name. In terms of human wisdom, he was a Perfect Fool. And if you think you can follow him without making something like the same kind of a fool of yourself, you are laboring under not a cross but a delusion.

There are two kinds of fools in the world: damned fools, and what Saint Paul calls "fools for Christ's sake" (1 Corinthians 4:10).

FORGIVENESS

To forgive somebody is to say one way or another, "You have done something unspeakable, and by all rights I should call it quits between us. Both my pride and my principles (q.v.) demand no less. However, although I make no guarantees that I will be able to forget what you've done, and though we may both carry the scars for life, I refuse to let it stand between us. I still want you for my friend."

To accept forgiveness means to admit that you've done something unspeakable that needs to be forgiven, and thus both parties must swallow the same thing: their pride.

This seems to explain what Jesus means when he says to God, "Forgive us our trespasses as we forgive those who trespass against us." Jesus is *not* saying that God's forgiveness is conditional upon our forgiving others. In the first place, forgiveness that's conditional isn't really forgiveness at all, just Fair Warning; and in the second place, our unforgivingness is among those things about us which we need to have God forgive us most. What Jesus apparently *is* saying is that the pride which keeps us from forgiving is the same pride which keeps us from accepting forgiveness, and will God please help us do something about it.

When somebody you've wronged forgives you, you're spared the dull and self-diminishing throb of a guilty conscience.

When you forgive somebody who has wronged you, you're spared the dismal corrosion of bitterness and wounded pride.

For both parties, forgiveness means the freedom again to be at peace inside their own skins and to be glad in each other's presence.

FREEDOM

We have freedom to the degree that the master whom we obey grants it to us in return for our obedience. We do well to choose a master in terms of how much freedom we get for how much obedience.

To obey the law of the land leaves us our constitutional freedom but not the freedom to follow our own consciences wherever they lead.

To obey the dictates of our own consciences leaves us freedom from the sense of moral guilt but not the freedom to gratify our own strongest appetites.

To obey our strongest appetites for drink, sex, power, revenge, or whatever leaves us the freedom of an animal to take what we want when we want it, but not the freedom of a human being to be human.

The old prayer speaks of God "in whose service is perfect freedom." The paradox is not as opaque as it sounds. It means that to obey Love himself, who above all else wishes us well, leaves us the freedom to be the best and gladdest that we have it in us to become. The only freedom Love denies us is the freedom to destroy ourselves ultimately. (*See also* HELL.)

Gg

GLORY

Glory is to God what style is to an artist. A painting by Vermeer, a sonnet by Donne, a Mozart aria—each is so rich with the style of the one who made it that to the connoisseur it couldn't have been made by anybody else, and the effect is staggering. The style of artists brings you as close to the sound of their voices and the light in their eyes as it is possible to get this side of actually shaking hands with them.

In the words of the nineteenth Psalm, "The heavens are telling the glory of God." It is the same thing. To the connoisseur, not just sunsets and starry nights but dust storms, rain forests, garter snakes, the human face, are all unmistakably the work of a single hand. Glory is the outward manifestation of that hand in its handiwork just as holiness (q.v.) is the inward. To behold God's glory, to sense his style, is the closest you can get to him this side of Paradise, just as to read *King Lear* is the closest you can get to Shakespeare.

Glory is what God looks like when for the time being all you have to look at him with is a pair of eyes.

GLUTTONY

A glutton is one who raids the icebox for a cure for spiritual malnutrition.

GOD

There must be a God because (a) since the beginning of history, the most variegated majority of people have intermittently believed there was; (b) it is hard to consider the vast and complex structure of the universe in general and of the human mind in particular without considering the possibility that they issued from some ultimate source, itself vast, complex, and somehow mindful; (c) built into the very being of even the most primitive man there seems to be a profound psychophysical need or hunger for something like truth, goodness, love, and—under one alias or another—for God; and (d) every age and culture has produced mystics who have experienced a Reality beyond reality and have come back using different words and images but obviously and without collusion describing with awed adoration the same Indescribability.

Statements of this sort and others like them have been advanced for several thousand years as proofs of the existence of God. A twelve-year-old child can see that no one of them is watertight. And even all of them taken together won't convince any of us unless our predisposition to be convinced outweighs our predisposition not to be.

It is as impossible to prove or disprove that God exists beyond the various and conflicting ideas people have dreamed up about him as it is to prove or disprove that Goodness exists beyond the various and conflicting ideas people have dreamed up about what is good.

It is as impossible for us to demonstrate the existence of God as it would be for even Sherlock Holmes to demonstrate the existence of Arthur Conan Doyle.

All-wise. All-powerful. All-loving. All-knowing. We bore to death both God and ourselves with our chatter. God cannot be expressed but only experienced.

In the last analysis, you cannot pontificate but can only point. A Christian is one who points at Christ and says, "I can't prove a thing, but there's something about his eyes and his voice. There's something about the way he carries his head, his hands. The way he carries his cross. The way he carries me." (*See also* RELIGION.)

GOSPEL

As everybody knows by now, Gospel means Good News. Ironically, it is some of the Gospel's most ardent fans who try to turn it into Bad News. For instance:

- "It all boils down to the Golden Rule. Just love thy neighbor, and that's all you have to worry about." *What makes this bad news is that loving our neighbor is exactly what none of us is very good at. Most of the time, we have a hard time even loving our family and friends very effectively.*
- "Jesus was a great teacher and the best example we have of how we ought to live." *As a teacher, Jesus is at least matched by, for instance, Siddhartha Gautama. As an example, we can only look at Jesus and despair.*
- "The Resurrection is a poetic way of saying that the spirit of Jesus lives on as a constant inspiration to us all." *If all the Resurrection means is that Jesus' spirit lives on like Abraham Lincoln's or Adolf Hitler's but that otherwise he is just as dead as anybody else who cashed in two thousand years ago, then, as Saint Paul puts it, "our preaching is in vain and your faith is in vain"* (1 Corinthians 15:14). *If the enemies of Jesus succeeded for all practical purposes in killing him permanently around* A.D. *30, then like Socrates, Thomas More, Dietrich Bonhoeffer, Martin Luther King, Jr., and so on, he is simply another saintly victim of the wickedness and folly of humankind, and the cross is a symbol of ultimate defeat.*

What is both Good and New about the Good News is the wild claim that Jesus did not simply tell us that God loves us even in our wickedness and folly and wants us to love each other the same way and to love him too, but that if we will let him, God will actually bring about this unprecedented transformation of our hearts himself.

What is both Good and New about the Good News is the mad insistence that Jesus lives on among us not just as another haunting memory but as the outlandish, holy, and invisible power of God working not just through the sacraments (q.v.) but in countless hidden ways to make even slobs like us loving and whole beyond anything we could conceivably pull off by ourselves.

Thus the Gospel is not only Good and New but, if you take it seriously, a Holy Terror. Jesus never claimed that the process of being changed from a slob into a human being was going to be a Sunday school picnic. On the contrary. Childbirth may occasionally be painless, but rebirth never. Part of what it means to be a slob is to hang on for dear life to our slobbery.

GRACE

After centuries of handling and mishandling, most religious words have become so shopworn nobody's much interested anymore. Not so with *grace*, for some reason. Mysteriously, even derivatives like *gracious* and *graceful* still have some of the bloom left.

Grace is something you can never get but can only be given. There's no way to earn it or deserve it or bring it about any more than you can deserve the taste of raspberries and cream or earn good looks or bring about your own birth.

A good sleep is grace and so are good dreams. Most tears are grace. The smell of rain is grace. Somebody loving you is grace. Loving somebody is grace. Have you ever *tried* to love somebody?

A crucial eccentricity of the Christian faith is the assertion that people are saved by grace. There's nothing *you* have to do. There's nothing you *have* to do. There's nothing you have to *do*.

The grace of God means something like: Here is your life. You might never have been, but you *are* because the party wouldn't have been complete without you. Here is the world. Beautiful and terrible things will happen. Don't be afraid. I am with you. Nothing can ever separate us. It's for you I created the universe. I love you.

There's only one catch. Like any other gift, the gift of grace can be yours only if you'll reach out and take it.

Maybe being able to reach out and take it is a gift too. (*See also* JUSTIFICATION.)

GUILT

Guilt is the responsibility for wrongdoing. Apart from the wrong we are each of us responsible for personally, in a sense no wrong is done anywhere which we are not all of us responsible for collectively. With or without knowing it, either through what we have done or what we have failed to do, we have all helped create the kind of world mess that makes wrongdoing inevitable.

The danger of our guilt, both personal and collective, is less that we won't take it to heart than that we'll take it to heart overmuch and let it fester there in ways that we ourselves often fail to recognize. We condemn in others the wrong we don't want to face in ourselves. We grow vindictive against the right for showing up our wrong as wrong. The sense of our own inner brokenness estranges us from the very ones who could help patch us together again. We steer clear of setting things right with the people we have wronged since their mere presence is a thorn in our flesh. Our desire to be clobbered for our guilt and thus rid of it tempts us to do things we will be clobbered for. The dismal variations are endless. More often than not, guilt is not merely the consequence of wrongdoing but the extension of it.

It is about as hard to absolve yourself of your own guilt as it is to sit in your own lap. Wrongdoing sparks guilt sparks wrongdoing *ad nauseum*, and we all try to disguise the grim process from both ourselves and everybody else. In order to break the circuit we need friends before whom we can put aside the disguise, trusting that when they see us for what we fully are, they won't run away screaming with, if nothing worse, laughter. Our trust in them leads us to trust their trust in us. In their presence the fact of our guilt no longer makes us feel and act out our guiltiness. For a moment at least the vicious circle stops circling and we can step down onto the firm ground of their acceptance, where maybe we'll be able to walk a straight line again. "Your sins are forgiven," Jesus said to the paralytic, then "Rise," whereupon the man picked up his bed and went home (Matthew 9:2–7).

Hh

HEALING

The Gospels depict Jesus as having spent a surprising amount of time healing people. Although, like the author of Job before him, he specifically rejected the theory that sickness was God's way of getting even with sinners (John 9:1–3), he nonetheless seems to have suggested a connection between sickness and sin, almost to have seen sin as a kind of sickness. "Those who are well have no need of a physician, but those who are sick," he said. "I came not to call the righteous but sinners" (Mark 2:17).

This is entirely compatible, of course, with the Hebrew view of the human being as a psychosomatic unity, an indivisible amalgam of body and soul whereby if either goes wrong, the other is affected. It is significant also that the Greek verb *sōzō* was used in Jesus' day to mean both to save and to heal, and *sŏ-tĕr* could signify either savior or physician.

Ever since the time of Jesus, healing has been part of the Christian tradition. In this century, it has usually been associated with religious quackery or the lunatic fringe; but as the psychosomatic dimension of disease has come to be taken more and more seriously by medical science, it has regained some of its former respectability. How nice for God to have this support at last.

Jesus is reported to have made the blind see and the lame walk, and over the centuries countless miraculous healings have been claimed in his name. For those who prefer not to believe in them, a number of approaches are possible, among them:

1. The idea of miracles is an offense both to our reason and to our dignity. Thus, *a priori,* miracles don't happen.
2. Unless there is objective medical evidence to substantiate the claim that a miraculous healing has happened, you can assume it hasn't.
3. If the medical authorities agree that a healing is inexplicable in terms of present scientific knowledge, you can simply ascribe this to the deficiencies of present scientific knowledge.
4. If otherwise intelligent and honest human beings are convinced, despite all arguments to the contrary, that it is God who has healed them, you can assume that their sickness, like its cure, was purely psychological. Whatever that means.
5. The crutches piled high at Lourdes and elsewhere are a monument to human humbug and credulity.

If your approach to this kind of healing is less ideological and more empirical, you can always give it a try. Pray for it. If it's somebody else's healing you're praying for, you can try at the same time laying your hands on her as Jesus sometimes did. If her sickness involves her body as well as her soul, then God may be able to use your inept hands as well as your inept faith to heal her.

If you feel like a fool as you are doing this, don't let it throw you. You are a fool, of course, only not a damned fool for a change.

If your prayer isn't answered, this may tell you more about you and your prayer than it does about God. Don't try too hard to feel religious, to generate some healing power of your own. Think of yourself instead (if you have to think of yourself at all) as a rather small-gauge, clogged-up pipe that a little of God's power may be able to filter through if you can just stay loose enough. Tell the one you're praying for to stay loose too.

If God doesn't seem to be giving you what you ask, maybe he's giving you something else. (*See also* PRAYER.)

HEAVEN (*See* ETERNAL LIFE)

HELL

People are free in this world to live for themselves alone if they want to and let the rest go hang, and they are free to live out the dismal consequences as long as they can stand it. The doctrine of Hell proclaims that they retain this same freedom in whatever world comes next. Thus the possibility of making damned fools of ourselves would appear to be limitless.

Or maybe Hell is the limit. Since the damned are said to suffer as dismally in the next world as they do in this one, they must still have enough life left in them to suffer with, which means that in their flight from Love, God apparently stops them just this side of extinguishing themselves utterly. Thus the bottomless pit is not really bottomless. Hell is the bottom beyond which God in his terrible mercy will not let them go.

Dante saw written over the gates of Hell the words "Abandon all hope ye who enter here," but he must have seen wrong. If there is suffering life in Hell, there must also be hope in Hell, because where there is life there is the Lord and giver of life; and where there is suffering he is there too, because the suffering of the ones he loves is also his suffering.

"He descended into Hell," the Creed says, and "If I make my bed in Sheol, thou art there," says the Psalmist (139:8). It seems there is no depth to which he will not sink. Maybe not even Old Scratch will be able to hold out against him forever.

HERETICS

Heretics are people who hold opinions at variance with established religious beliefs. In the old days, they were burned at the stake. Their books were banned. Wars were fought against them. They were an endangered species. As time passed, they grew to be so much in the majority that the tables have turned, and now what's in danger are established religious beliefs.

It's not that the opinions of heretics on matters like the Trinity, the Sacraments, and the Divinity of Jesus are at variance with orthodoxy but that they have few if any opinions on such matters at all because such matters strike them as utterly irrelevant to the human condition. They're no longer out to bring the Church around to their way of thinking because by and large they're about as interested in what the Church thinks as they are in how many angels could dance on the head of a pin if there were such things as angels.

Modern-day heretics are less opposed to religion than they are simply left cold by it, and when you consider how the Church more often than not proclaims the Gospel—either passionlessly and unconvincingly or flamboyantly and phonily—it is no great wonder.

HISTORY

Unlike Buddhism or Hinduism, biblical faith takes history very seriously because God takes it very seriously. He took it seriously enough to begin it and to enter it and to promise that one day he will bring it to a serious close. The biblical view is that history is not an absurdity to be endured or an illusion to be dispelled or an endlessly repeating cycle to be escaped. Instead it is for each of us a series of crucial, precious, and unrepeatable moments that are seeking to lead us somewhere.

The true history of humankind and the true history of each individual has less to do than we tend to think with the kind of information that gets into most histories, biographies, and autobiographies. True history has to do with the saving and losing of souls, and both of these are apt to take place when most people—including the one whose soul is at stake—are looking the other way. The real turning point in our lives is less likely to be the day we win the election or get married than the morning we decide not to mail the letter or the afternoon we watch the woods fill up with snow. The real turning point in human history is less apt to be the day the wheel is invented or Rome falls than the day a boy is born to a couple of Jews.

HOLY

Only God is holy, just as only people are human. God's holiness is his Godness. To speak of anything else as holy is to say that it has something of God's mark upon it. Times, places, things, and people can all be holy, and when they are, they are usually not hard to recognize.

One holy place I know is a workshop attached to a barn. There is a wood-burning stove in it made out of an oil drum. There is a workbench, dark and dented, with shallow, crammed drawers behind one of which a cat lives. There is a girlie calendar on the wall, plus various lengths of chain and rope, shovels and rakes of different sizes and shapes, some worn-out jackets and caps on pegs, an electric clock that doesn't keep time. On the workbench are two small plug-in radios, both of which have serious things wrong with them. There are several metal boxes full of wrenches, and a bench saw. There are a couple of chairs with rungs missing. There is an old yellow bulldozer with its tracks caked with mud parked against one wall. The place smells mainly of engine oil and smoke—both wood smoke and pipe smoke. The windows are small, and even on bright days what light there is comes through mainly in window-sized patches on the floor.

I have no idea why this place is holy, but you can tell it is the moment you set foot in it if you have an eye for that kind of thing. For reasons known only to God, it is one of the places he uses for sending his love to the world through.

HOLY COMMUNION (*See* LORD'S SUPPER)

HOLY SPIRIT (*See* SPIRIT, TRINITY)

HOMELESSNESS

We lie in our beds in the dark. There is a picture of the children on the bureau. A patch of moonlight catches our clothes thrown over the back of a chair. We can hear the faint rumble of the furnace in the cellar. We are surrounded by the reassurance of the familiar. When the weather is bad, we have shelter. When things are bad in our lives, we have a place where we can retreat to lick our wounds while tens of thousands of people, many of them children, wander the dark streets in search of some corner to lie down in out of the wind.

Yet we are homeless even so in the sense of having homes but not being really at home in them. To be really at home is to be really at peace, and there can be no real peace for any of us until there is some measure of real peace for all of us. When we close our eyes to the deep needs of other people whether they live on the streets or under our own roof—and when we close our eyes to our own deep need to reach out to them—we can never be fully at home anywhere.

HOPE (*See* WISHFUL THINKING, CROSS)

For Christians, hope is ultimately hope in Christ. The hope that he really is what for centuries we have been claiming he is. The hope that despite the fact that sin and death still rule the world, he somehow conquered them. The hope that in him and through him all of us stand a chance of somehow conquering them too. The hope that at some unforeseeable time and in some unimaginable way he will return with healing in his wings.

No one in the New Testament calls a spade a spade as unflinchingly as Saint Paul. "If Christ has not been raised, your faith is futile," he wrote to the Corinthians. "If for this life only we have hoped in Christ, we are of all people most to be pitied" (1 Corinthians 15:17, 19). That is the possibility in spite of which Saint Paul and the rest of us go on hoping even so. That is the possibility which led Dostoyevski to write to a friend, "If anyone proved to me that Christ was outside the truth, and it really was so that the truth was outside Christ, then I would prefer to remain with Christ than with the truth."

HUMANKIND

Humans are so the universe will have something to talk through, so God will have something to talk with, and so the rest of us will have something to talk about.

The biblical view of the history of humankind and of each individual man or woman is contained in the first three chapters of Genesis. We are created to serve God by loving him and each other in freedom and joy, but we invariably choose bondage and woe instead as prices not too high to pay for independence. To say that God drove Adam and Eve out of Eden is apparently a euphemism for saying that Adam and Eve, like the rest of us, made a break for it as soon as God happened to look the other way. If God really wanted to get rid of us, the chances are he wouldn't have kept hounding us every step of the way ever since. (*See also* HISTORY, JUSTIFICATION.)

HUMILITY

Humility is often confused with the polite self-deprecation of saying you're not much of a bridge player when you know perfectly well you are. Conscious or otherwise, this kind of humility is a form of gamesmanship.

If you really *aren't* much of a bridge player, you're apt to be rather proud of yourself for admitting it so humbly. This kind of humility is a form of low comedy.

True humility doesn't consist of thinking ill of yourself but of not thinking of yourself much differently from the way you'd be apt to think of anybody else. It is the capacity for being no more and no less pleased when you play your own hand well than when your opponents do. (*See also* PRIDE.)

Ii

IDOLATRY

Idolatry is the practice of ascribing absolute value to things of relative worth. Under certain circumstances, money, patriotism, sexual freedom, moral principles, family loyalty, physical beauty, social or intellectual preeminence, and so on are fine things to have around; but to make them the standard by which all other values are measured, to make them your masters, to look to them to justify your life and save your soul is sheerest folly. They just aren't up to it.

Idolatry is always popular among religious people, but idols made out of things like the Denomination, the Bible, the Liturgy, the Holy Images, are apt to seem so limited in real power even to their idolaters that there is always the hope that in time they will overthrow themselves.

It is among the unreligious that idolatry is a particular menace. Having ushered God out once and for all through the front door, the unbeliever is under constant temptation to replace him with something spirited in through the service entrance. From the moment the eighteenth-century French revolutionaries set up the Goddess of Reason on the high altar of Notre Dame, there wasn't a head in all Paris that was safe.

IMMORTALITY

Immortal means death-proof. To believe in the immortality of the soul is to believe that though John Brown's body lies a-moldering in the grave, his soul goes marching on simply because marching on is the nature of souls just the way producing butterflies is the nature of caterpillars. Bodies die, but souls don't.

True or false, this is not the biblical view, although many who ought to know better assume it is. The biblical view differs in several significant ways:

1. As someone has put it, the biblical understanding of human beings is not that they *have* bodies, but that they *are* bodies. When God made Adam, he did it by slapping some mud together to make a body and then breathing some breath into it to make a living soul. Thus the body and soul which make up human beings are as inextricably part and parcel of each other as the leaves and flames that make up a bonfire. When you kick the bucket, you kick it one hundred percent. All of you. There is nothing left to go marching on with.

2. The idea that the body dies and the soul doesn't is an idea which implies that the body is something rather gross and embarrassing, like a case of hemorrhoids. The Greeks spoke of it as the prison house of the soul. The suggestion was that to escape it altogether was something less than a disaster.

The Bible, on the other hand, sees the body in particular and the material world in general as a good and glorious invention. How could it be otherwise when it was invented by a good and glorious God?

The Old Testament rings loud with the praises of trees and birds and rain and mountains, of wine that gladdens the heart of man and oil that makes his face shine and bread that strengthens him. Read the 104th Psalm for instance. Or try the Song of Solomon for as abandoned and unabashed a celebration of the physical as you're apt to find anywhere.

As for the New Testament, Jesus himself, far from being a world-denying ascetic, was accused of being a wino and a chowhound (Matthew 11:19).

When he heard that his friend Lazarus was dead, he didn't mouth any pious clichés about what a merciful release it was. He wept.

The whole idea of incarnation (q.v.), of the word becoming flesh, affirms the physical and fleshly in yet another way, by declaring that it was a uniform God himself wasn't ashamed to wear.

Saint Paul undoubtedly had his hang-ups, but when he compares flesh unfavorably to spirit, he is not talking about body versus soul, but about the old person without Christ versus the new person with him.

3. Those who believe in the immortality of the soul believe that life after death is as natural a human function as waking after sleep.

The Bible instead speaks of resurrection. It is entirely unnatural. We do not go on living beyond the grave because that's how we are made. Rather, we go to our graves as dead as a doornail and are given our lives back again by God (i.e., resurrected) just as we were given them by God in the first place, because that is the way God is made.

4. All the major Christian creeds affirm belief in resurrection *of the body.* In other words, they affirm the belief that what God in spite of everything prizes enough to bring back to life is not just some disembodied echo of human beings but a new and revised version of all the things which made them the particular human beings they were and which they need something like a body to express: their personality, the way they looked, the sound of their voices, their peculiar capacity for creating and loving, in some sense their *faces*.

5. The idea of the immortality of the soul is based on the experience of humanity's indomitable spirit. The idea of the

resurrection of the body is based on the experience of God's unspeakable love.

INCARNATION

"The Word became flesh," wrote John, "and dwelt among us, full of grace and truth" (John 1:14). That is what incarnation means. It is untheological. It is unsophisticated. It is undignified. But according to Christianity, it is the way things are.

All religions and philosophies which deny the reality or the significance of the material, the fleshly, the earthbound, are themselves denied. Moses at the burning bush was told to take off his shoes because the ground on which he stood was holy ground (Exodus 3:5), and incarnation means that all ground is holy ground because God not only made it but walked on it, ate and slept and worked and died on it. If we are saved anywhere, we are saved here. And what is saved is not some diaphanous distillation of our bodies and our earth, but our bodies and our earth themselves. Jerusalem becomes the New Jerusalem coming down out of heaven like a bride adorned for her husband (Revelation 21:2). Our bodies are sown perishable and raised imperishable (1 Corinthians 15:42).

One of the blunders religious people are particularly fond of making is the attempt to be more spiritual than God.

ISRAEL

As soon as God decided to take a hand in history, he had to start somewhere. What he elected to start with was Israel. This election has been a constant source of dismay, delight, and embarrassment to them both ever since. The account of the first few millennia of their stormy affair is contained in the Old Testament.

When Israel asked the question why God elected them, of all people, they arrived at two main answers. One answer was that God elected them for special privilege, but the tragic course of their own history soon disabused them of that. The other answer was that he elected them for terrible responsibility.

When Israel asked the question what the responsibility was that God had saddled them with, they arrived at two main answers. One answer was that their responsibility was to impose upon the world the knowledge of the One True God—but they were never very successful in doing that. The other answer was that their responsibility was to suffer and die for the world.

None of them wanted to suffer and die very much, including Jesus, but Jesus did it anyway. It was only afterward that people began to understand why this was necessary, although nobody has ever explained it very well and Jesus himself never seems to have tried. When Jesus died, something happened in the lives of certain people that made explanations as unnecessary as they were inevitable, and it has gone on happening ever since.

Jj

JESUS

According to John, the last words Jesus spoke from the cross were, "It is finished." Whether he meant "finished" as brought to an end, in the sense of finality, or "finished" as brought to completion, in the sense of fulfillment, nobody knows. Maybe he meant both.

What was brought to an end was of course nothing less than his life. The Gospels make no bones about that. He died as dead as any man. All the days of his life led him to this day, and beyond this day there would be no other days, and he knew it. It was finished now, he said. He was finished. He had come to the last of all his moments, and because he was conscious still—alive to his death—maybe, as they say the dying do, he caught one final glimpse of the life he had all but finished living.

Who knows what he glimpsed as that life passed before him. Maybe here and there a fragment preserved for no good reason like old snapshots in a desk drawer: the play of sunlight on a wall, a half-remembered face, something somebody said. A growing sense perhaps of destiny: the holy man in the river, a gift for prayer, a gift for moving simple hearts. One hopes he remembered good times, although the Gospels record few—how he once fell asleep in a boat as a storm was coming up, and how he went to a wedding where water was the least of what was turned into wine. Then the failures of the last days, when only a handful gathered to watch him enter the city on the foal of an ass—and those very likely for the wrong reasons. The terror that he himself had known for a few moments in the garden, and that finally drove even the handful away. *Shalom* then, the God in him moving his swollen lips to forgive them all, to forgive maybe even God. Finished.

What was brought to completion by such a life and such a death only he can know now, wherever he is, if he is anywhere. The *Christ* of it is beyond our imagining. All we can know is the flesh and blood of it, the *Jesus* of it. In that sense, what was completed was at the very least a hope to live by, a mystery to hide our faces before, a shame to haunt us, a dream of holiness to help make bearable our night.

JEWELS

"You were in Eden, the garden of God; every precious stone was your covering," the Lord said to the King of Tyre, "carnelian, topaz, and jasper, chrysolite, beryl, and onyx; sapphire, carbuncle, and emerald." But then, as the Lord goes on to explain, because the King fell from innocence into sin, "I cast you as a profane thing from the mountain of God, and the guardian cherub drove you out from the midst of the stones of fire" (Ezekiel 28:13, 16).

One way or another, we have all fallen like the King. Yet we all also carry within us a memory of Eden. It is perhaps why jewels fascinate us so and why we value them above almost all things. In their starry depths we see glimmers of where we have come from and also of where, according to ancient prophecy, we are going: the city whose "walls are . . . chrysoprase . . . jacinth . . . amethyst . . . and the twelve gates . . . twelve pearls . . . and the street . . . gold" (Revelation 21:19–21 *passim*).

JOB

Job is a good man and knows it, as does everybody else, including God. Then one day his cattle are stolen, his servants are killed, and the wind blows down the house where his children happen to be whooping it up at the time, and not one of them lives to tell what it was they thought they had to whoop it up about. But being a good man he says only, "The Lord gave, and the Lord hath taken away. Blessed be the name of the Lord." Even when he comes down with a bad case of boils and his wife advises him to curse God and die, he manages to bite his tongue and say nothing. It's his friends who finally break the camel's back. They come to offer their condolences and hang around a full week. When Job finds them still there at the start of the second week, he curses the day he was born. He never quite takes his wife's advice and curses God, but he comes very close to it. He asks some unpleasant questions:

If God is all he's cracked up to be, how come houses blow down on innocent people? Why does a good woman die of cancer in her prime while an old man who can't remember his name or hold his water goes on in a nursing home forever? Why are there so many crooks riding around in Cadillacs and so many children going to bed hungry at night? Job's friends offer an assortment of theological explanations, but God doesn't offer one.

God doesn't explain. He explodes. He asks Job who he thinks he is anyway. He says that to try to explain the kinds of things Job wants explained would be like trying to explain Einstein to a little-neck clam. He also, incidentally, gets off some of the greatest poetry in the Old Testament. "Hast thou entered into the treasures of the snow? Canst thou bind the sweet influences of the Pleiades? Hast thou given the horse strength and clothed his neck with thunder?"

Maybe the reason God doesn't explain to Job why terrible things happen is that he knows what Job needs isn't an explanation. Suppose that God did explain. Suppose that God were to say to Job that the reason the cattle were stolen, the crops ruined, and the children killed was thus and so, spelling everything out right down to and including the case of boils. Job would have his explanation.

And then what?

Understanding in terms of the divine economy why his children had to die, Job would still have to face their empty chairs at breakfast every morning. Carrying in his pocket straight from the horse's mouth a complete theological justification of his boils, he would still have to scratch and burn.

God doesn't reveal his grand design. He reveals himself. He doesn't show why things are as they are. He shows his face. And Job says, "I had heard of thee by the hearing of the ear, but now my eyes see thee." Even covered with sores and ashes, he looks oddly like a man who has asked for a crust and been given the whole loaf.

At least for the moment.

JOKE

Many ministers include in their sermons a joke or two which may or may not be relevant to what the sermons are about but in any case are supposed to warm up the congregation and demonstrate that preachers are just plain folks like everybody else.

There are two dangers in this. One is that if the joke is a good one, the chances are it will be the only part of the sermon that anybody remembers on Monday morning. The other is that when preachers tell jokes, it is often an unconscious way of telling both their congregations and themselves that the Gospel is all very well but in the last analysis not to be taken too seriously.

JOY

In the Gospel of John, Jesus sums up pretty much everything by saying, "These things I have spoken to you, that my joy may be in you, and that your joy may be full" (John 15:11). He said it at the supper that he knew was the last one he'd have a mouth to eat.

Happiness turns up more or less where you'd expect it to—a good marriage, a rewarding job, a pleasant vacation. Joy, on the other hand, is as notoriously unpredictable as the one who bequeaths it.

JUDGMENT

We are all of us judged every day. We are judged by the face that looks back at us from the bathroom mirror. We are judged by the faces of the people we love and by the faces and lives of our children and by our dreams. We are judged by the faces of the people we do not love. Each day finds us at the junction of many roads, and we are judged as much by the roads we have not taken as by the roads we have.

The New Testament proclaims that at some unforeseeable time in the future, God will ring down the final curtain on history, and there will come a Day on which all our days and all the judgments upon us and all our judgments upon each other will themselves be judged. The judge will be Christ. In other words, the one who judges us most finally will be the one who loves us most fully.

Romantic love is blind to everything except what is lovable and lovely, but Christ's love sees us with terrible clarity and sees us whole. Christ's love so wishes our joy that it is ruthless against everything in us that diminishes our joy. The worst sentence Love can pass is that we behold the suffering which Love has endured for our sake, and that is also our acquittal. The justice and mercy of the judge are ultimately one.

JUSTIFICATION

In printers' language, to "justify" means to set type in such a way that all full lines are of equal length and flush both left and right; in other words, to put the printed lines in the right relationship with the page they're printed on and with each other. The religious sense of the word is very close to this. Being justified means being brought into right relation. Paul says simply that being justified means having peace with God (Romans 5:1). He uses the noun "justification" for the first step in the process of salvation (q.v.).

During his Pharisee phase or "blue period," Paul was on his way to Damascus to mop up some Christians when suddenly he heard the voice of Jesus Christ, whose resurrection he had up till now considered only an ugly rumor. What he might have expected the voice to say was, "Just you wait." What in effect it did say was, "I want you on my side." Paul never got over it.

As far as Paul was concerned, he was the last man in the world for God to have called this way, but God had, thereby revealing himself to be a God who was willing to do business with you even if you were in the process of mopping up Christians at the time. Paul also discovered that all the Brownie points he had been trying to rack up as a super-Pharisee had been pointless. God did business with you not because of who you were but because of who he was.

All the Voice seemed to want Paul to do was believe that it meant what it said and do as it asked. Paul did both.

At a moment in his life when he had least reason to expect it, Paul was staggered by the idea that no matter who you are or what you've done, God wants you on his side. There is nothing you have to do or be. It's on the house. It goes with the territory. God has "justified you," lined you up. To feel this somehow in your bones is the first step on the way to being saved.

You don't have to hear a Voice on the road to Damascus to feel it in your bones either. Maybe just noticing that the sun shines every bit as bright and sweet on Jack the Ripper as it does on Little Orphan Annie will do the trick. Maybe just noticing the holy and hallowing givenness of your own life.

Kk

KINGDOM OF GOD

It is not a place, of course, but a condition. *Kingship* might be a better word. "Thy kingdom come, thy will be done," Jesus prayed. The two are in apposition.

Insofar as here and there, and now and then, God's kingly will is being done in various odd ways among us even at this moment, the kingdom has come already.

Insofar as all the odd ways we do his will at this moment are at best half-baked and halfhearted, the kingdom is still a long way off—a hell of a long way off, to be more precise and theological.

As a poet, Jesus is maybe at his best in describing the feeling you get when you glimpse the Thing Itself—the kingship of the king official at last and all the world his coronation. It's like finding a million dollars in a field, he says, or a jewel worth a king's ransom. It's like finding something you hated to lose and thought you'd never find again—an old keepsake, a stray sheep, a missing child. When the kingdom really comes, it's as if the thing you lost and thought you'd never find again is you. (*See also* ETERNAL LIFE.)

Ll

LAUGHTER (*See* FAITH, ATHEIST)

LAW

There are basically two kinds: (1) law as the way things ought to be, and (2) law as the way things are. An example of the first is NO TRESPASSING. An example of the second is the law of gravity.

God's Law has traditionally been spelled out in terms of category No. 1, a compendium of do's and don'ts. These do's and don'ts are the work of moralists and when obeyed serve the useful purpose of keeping us from each other's throats. They can't make us human but they can help keep us honest.

God's Law *in itself*, however, comes under category No. 2 and is the work of God. It has been stated in eight words: "He who does not love remains in death" (1 John 3:14). Like it or not, that's how it is. If you don't believe it, you can always put it to the test just the way if you don't believe the law of gravity, you can always step out a tenth-story window. (*See also* MORALITY.)

LIFE

The temptation is always to reduce it to size. A bowl of cherries. A rat race. Amino acids. Even to call it *a* mystery smacks of reductionism. It is *the* mystery.

As far as anybody seems to know, the vast majority of things in the universe do not have whatever life is. Sticks, stones, stars, space—they simply *are*. A few things *are* and are somehow alive to it. They have broken through into Something, or Something has broken through into them. Even a jellyfish, a butternut squash. They're in it with us. We're all in it together, or it in us. Life is *it*. Life is *with*.

After lecturing learnedly on miracles, a great theologian was asked to give a specific example of one. "There is only one miracle," he answered. "It is life."

Have you wept at anything during the past year?

Has your heart beat faster at the sight of young beauty?

Have you thought seriously about the fact that someday you are going to die?

More often than not, do you really *listen* when people are speaking to you instead of just waiting for your turn to speak?

Is there anybody you know in whose place, if one of you had to suffer great pain, you would volunteer yourself?

If your answer to all or most of these questions is No, the chances are that you're dead.

LIGHT

We can't see light itself. We can see only what light lights up, like the little circle of night where the candle flickers—a sheen of mahogany, a wineglass, a face leaning toward us out of the shadows.

When Jesus says that he is the Light of the World (John 8:12), maybe something like that is part of what he is saying. He himself is beyond our seeing, but in the darkness where we stand, we see, thanks to him, something of the path that stretches out from the door, something of whatever it is that keeps us trying more or less to follow the path even when we can hardly believe that it goes anywhere worth going or that we have what it takes to go there, something of whoever it is that every once in a while seems to lean toward us out of the shadows.

LORD'S SUPPER

It is make-believe. You make believe that the one who breaks the bread and blesses the wine is not the plump parson who smells of Williams' Aqua Velva but Jesus of Nazareth. You make believe that the tasteless wafer and cheap port are his flesh and blood. You make believe that by swallowing them you are swallowing his life into your life and that there is nothing in earth or heaven more important for you to do than this.

It is a game you play because he said to play it. "Do this in remembrance of me." Do *this*.

Play that it makes a difference. Play that it makes sense. If it seems a childish thing to do, do it in remembrance that you are a child.

Remember Max Beerbohm's Happy Hypocrite, the wicked man who wore the mask of a saint to woo and win the saintly girl he loved. Years later, when a castoff girlfriend discovered the ruse, she challenged him to take off the mask in front of his beloved and show his face for the sorry thing it was. He did what he was told, only to discover that underneath the saint's mask, his face had become the face of a saint.

This same reenactment of the Last Supper is sometimes called the Eucharist, from a Greek word meaning thanksgiving, i.e., at the Last Supper itself Christ gave thanks, and on their part, Christians have nothing for which to be more thankful.

It is also called the Mass from *missa,* the word of dismissal used at the end of the Latin service. It is the end. It is over. All those long prayers and aching knees. Now back into the fresh air. Back home. Sunday dinner. Now life can begin again. *Exactly.*

It is also called Holy Communion because when feeding at this implausible table, Christians believe that they are communing with the Holy One himself, his spirit enlivening their spirits, heating the blood and gladdening the heart just the way wine, as spirits, can (*see* WINE).

They are also, of course, communing with each other. To eat any meal together is to meet at the level of our most basic need. It is hard to preserve your dignity with butter on your chin, or to keep your distance when asking for the tomato ketchup.

To eat this particular meal together is to meet at the level of our most basic humanness, which involves our need not just for food but for each other (*see* BREAD). I need you to help fill my emptiness just as you need me to help fill yours. As for the emptiness that's still left over, well, we're in it together, or it in us. Maybe it's most of what makes us human and makes us brothers and sisters.

The next time you walk down the street, take a good look at every face you pass and in your mind say, *Christ died for thee.* That girl. That slob. That phony. That crook. That saint. That damned fool. *Christ* died for thee. Take and eat this in remembrance that Christ died for *thee.* (*See also* RITUAL, SACRAMENT.)

LOVE

The first stage is to believe that there is only one kind of love. The middle stage is to believe that there are many kinds of love and that the Greeks had a different word for each of them. The last stage is to believe that there is only one kind of love.

The unabashed *eros* of lovers, the sympathetic *philia* of friends, *agape* giving itself away freely no less for the murderer than for his victim (the King James version translates it as *charity*)—these are all varied manifestations of a single reality. To lose yourself in another's arms, or in another's company, or in suffering for all men who suffer, including the ones who inflict suffering upon you—to lose yourself in such ways is to find yourself. Is what it's all about. Is what love is.

Of all powers, love is the most powerful and the most powerless. It is the most powerful because it alone can conquer that final and most impregnable stronghold which is the human heart. It is the most powerless because it can do nothing except by consent.

To say that love is God is romantic idealism. To say that God is love is either the last straw or the ultimate truth.

In the Christian sense, love is not primarily an emotion, but an act of the will. When Jesus tells us to love our neighbors, he is not telling us to love them in the sense of responding to them with a cozy emotional feeling. You can as easily produce a cozy emotional feeling on demand as you can a yawn or a sneeze. On the contrary, he is telling us to love our neighbors in the sense of being willing to work for their well-being even if it means sacrificing our own well-being to that end, even if it means sometimes just leaving them alone. Thus in Jesus' terms, we can love our neighbors without necessarily liking them. In fact liking them may stand in the way of loving them by making us overprotective sentimentalists instead of reasonably honest friends.

When Jesus talked to the Pharisees, he didn't say, "There, there. Everything's going to be all right." He said, "You brood of vipers! how can you speak good when you are evil!" (Matthew 12:34). And he said that to them because he loved them.

This does not mean that liking may not be a part of loving, only that it doesn't have to be. Sometimes liking follows on the heels of loving. It is hard to work for people's well-being very long without coming in the end to rather like them too.

LUST

Lust is the craving for salt of a person who is dying of thirst.

LYING

There is perhaps nothing that so marks us as human as the gift of speech. Who knows to what degree and in what ways animals have the power to communicate with each other, but to all appearances it is only a shadow of ours. By speaking, we can reveal the hiddenness of thought, we can express the subtlest as well as the most devastating of emotions, we can heal, we can make poems, we can pray. All of which is to say we can speak truth—the truth of what it is to be ourselves, to be with each other, to be in the world—and such speaking as that is close to what being human is all about. What makes lying an evil is less that the world is mischievously deceived by it than that we are sorely dehumanized by it.

Mm

MAGIC

Magic is saying Abracadabra and pulling the rabbit out of the hat, is stepping on a crack to break your mother's back, is a dashboard Jesus to prevent smash-ups. Magic is going to church so you will get to Heaven. Magic is using Listerine so everybody will love you. Magic is the technique of controlling unseen powers and will always work if you do it by the book. Magic is manipulation and says, My will be done. Religion is propitiation and says, Thy will be done.

Religion is praying, and maybe the prayer will be answered and maybe it won't, at least not the way you want or when you want and maybe not at all. Even if you do it by the book, religion doesn't always work, as Jesus pointed out in one of his more somber utterances when he said, "Not everyone who says, 'Lord, Lord,' shall enter the kingdom of Heaven" (Matthew 7:21), the corollary to which would appear to be, "Not everyone who wouldn't be caught dead saying 'Lord, Lord,' shall be blackballed from the kingdom of Heaven." He softened the blow somewhat then by adding that the way to enter the kingdom of Heaven is to do the will of his Father in Heaven; but when religion claims that it's always sure what that will is, it's only bluffing. Magic is always sure.

If security's what you're after, try magic. If adventure is what you're after, try religion. The line between them is notoriously fuzzy.

MARY

"Behold, thy father and I have sought thee sorrowing," Mary said, as she and Joseph came upon Jesus at last in the Temple when he was a child (Luke 2:48); and in a sense it was her fate to seek him sorrowing ever after. She sorrowed perhaps because, following his own counsel, he left both mother and father in order to proclaim his dangerous Gospel; sorrowed because it would appear that she loved him too much for himself rather than for the Will he believed he was born both to serve and to embody; sorrowed because there is reason at least to suspect that like most of the others who were closest to him she never really understood what he was about and may have been one of those who, seeing the great danger he was in, tried to save him from the angry crowd by saying, "He is beside himself" (Mark 3:21).

It's possible that the words he spoke to her were not as harsh in Aramaic as they sound in English, yet even so it's hard to believe that they too didn't cause her some measure of sorrow. There was the time he said, "Woman, what have I to do with thee?" when she came to him at Cana about the wine (John 2:4). And there was the time he asked, "Who is my mother?" when he was told that she was outside waiting for him. "Whosoever shall do the will of my Father which is in heaven, the same is my . . . mother" (Matthew 12:46–50).

Sentiment would have it otherwise, but you can search in vain for some word of particular tenderness, some gesture of particular concern, for the one who bore him. It's as if he could not belong truly to any unless he belonged truly to all. They were all his mothers and brothers and sisters, and nowhere in the Gospels does he offer her any more than he offered everyone else.

Nowhere, that is, except at the very end, when he looked down at her from his torture. Even here he did not call her

Mother, only "woman," and there is no leave-taking to break her heart or ours. But it is as if here at last he spoke to the need that he must have always sensed in her. "Behold thy son," he said, and then to the beloved disciple, "Behold thy mother" (John 19:26–27), bequeathing to her the son that he himself had had no way of being, what with a world to save, a death to die. He would be present in the disciple, he seemed to say, for her to live for, and to live for her. Beyond that, he would be present in generation after generation for her to mother, the Mater Dolorosa who seeks him always, and sorrowing, in even the unlikeliest hearts.

MASS (*See* LORD'S SUPPER)

MEDITATION

In our minds we are continually chattering with ourselves, and the purpose of meditation is to stop it. To begin with, maybe we try to concentrate on a single subject—the flame of a candle, the row of peas we are weeding, our own breath. When other subjects float up to distract us, we escape them by simply taking note of them and then letting them float away without thinking about them. We keep returning to the in and out of our breathing until there is no room left in us for anything else. To the candle flame until we ourselves start to flicker and burn. To the peas until we become only a pair of grubby hands weeding them. In time we discover that we are no longer chattering.

If we persist, every once and so often we may find ourselves entering the suburbs of a state where we are conscious but no longer conscious of anything in particular, where we have let go of almost everything.

The end of meditation is to become empty enough to be filled with the kind of stillness the Psalmist has in mind when he says, "Be still, and know that I am God" (Psalm 46:10).

MEMORY

There are two ways of remembering. One way is to make an excursion from the living present back into the dead past. The old sock remembers how things used to be when you and I were young, Maggie. The faraway look in his eyes is partly the beer and partly that he's really far away.

The other way is to summon the dead past back into the living present. The young widow remembers her husband, and he is there beside her.

When Jesus said, "Do this in remembrance of me" (1 Corinthians 11:24), he was not prescribing a periodic slug of nostalgia.

MERCY (*See* JUDGMENT)

MESSIAH

Wie man's macht, ist's falsch is a crude German saying which means, freely translated, *Whatever men do, it turns out lousy.* The Russians throw out the tsars and end up with Stalin. The Americans free their slaves so they can move out into the ghettos, and they fight one of the most tragic and costly wars of their history so that South Vietnam can end up with a government that would have brought a blush to the cheeks of Boss Tweed.

Or take the Jews. The nation that God chooses to be the hope of the world becomes the stooge of the world. The nation of priests becomes a nation of international politicians so inept at playing one major power off against another that by the time they're through, Egypt, Assyria, Babylonia, Persia, Rome, all have a chance at wiping their feet on them—the cream of the population deported, the Temple destroyed, Jerusalem razed. The Law of Moses becomes the legalism of the Pharisees, and "Can mortal man be righteous before God?" becomes "Is it kosher to wear my dentures on the Sabbath?" The high priests sell out to the army of occupation. The Holy City turns into Miami Beach. Even God is fed up. Nobody knows all this better than the Jews know it. Who else has a Wailing Wall? Read the prophets.

Wie man's macht, ist's falsch. But the Jews went on hoping anyway, and beginning several centuries before the birth of Jesus, much of their hope took the form of an implausible dream that someday God in his fathomless mercy would send them Somebody to make everything right. He was referred to as the Messiah, which means in Hebrew the Anointed One, i.e., the One anointed by God, as a king at his coronation is anointed, only for a bigger job. The Greek word for Messiah is Christ.

How and when the Messiah would come was debatable. Theories as to what he would be like multiplied and overlapped: a great warrior king like David, a great priest like Melchizedek, a great prophet like Elijah. Who could possibly say? But whatever he was, his name would be called "Wonderful Counselor, Mighty God, Everlasting Father, Prince of Peace," and "of the increase of his government and of peace there would be no end" (Isaiah 9:6–7). Handel set him to music. On Passover eve to this day an extra cup is placed on the table for Elijah in case he stops in to say the Messiah is here at last. The door is left open.

When Jesus of Nazareth came riding into Jerusalem on his mule, a small group of radicals, illiterates, and ne'er-do-wells hailed him as the Messiah, the Christ. Everybody else suggested that you had to draw the line somewhere and advised as public and unpleasant an execution as possible so nobody would fail to get the point. No one can deny that reason and prudence were on the side of the latter.

Reasons for Drawing the Line Somewhere

1. He wasn't a king, a priest, or a prophet. He was Nobody from Nowhere. He spoke with an accent.

2. On the one hand, his attitude toward the Law was cavalier to say the least. He said that it wasn't what went into your mouth that mattered but what came out of it, thus setting back both the kosher industry and the WCTU about a

thousand years apiece (Matthew 15:11). Also, some of his best friends were whores and crooks.

3. On the other hand, he not only went further than Moses, but claimed his own to be the higher authority. Moses was against murder. Jesus was against vindictive anger. Moses was against adultery. Jesus was against recreational sex. Moses said love your neighbor. Jesus said love your enemy too. Moses said be good. Jesus said be perfect (Matthew 5:21–48).

4. Who did he think he was anyway?

5. Who *can* be perfect? (*See* SALVATION.)

6. Who wants to be?

7. He was not only a threat to the established church but to the Establishment itself. Jewish orthodoxy and the Pax Romana were both in danger. He could easily have become a Fidel Castro.

8. His fans attributed a great many miracles to him up to and including bringing a corpse back to life, but there was one miracle he couldn't pull off, and that was saving his own skin. He died just as dead on the cross as all the others who had died on it, and some of them held out a lot longer.

9. His fans continue to ascribe a great many miracles to him, including his own resurrection, but the world is in just about as bad shape since his time as before, maybe worse.

As far as I know there is only one good reason for believing that he was who he said he was. One of the crooks he was strung up with put it this way: "If you are the Christ, save yourself and us" (Luke 23:39). Save us from whatever we need most to be saved from. Save us from each other. Save us from ourselves. Save us from death both beyond the grave and before.

If he is, he can. If he isn't, he can't. It may be that the only way in the world to find out is to give him the chance, whatever that involves. It may be just as simple and just as complicated as that. (*See also* JESUS.)

MINISTER

There are three basic views:

1. Ministers are Nice People. They'll take a drink if you offer them one, and when it comes to racy stories, they can tell a few right along with the best of them. They preach good sermons, but they're not like those religious fanatics who think they've got to say a prayer every time they pay a call. When it comes to raising money, they're nobody's fool and have all the rich old parishioners eating out of their hands. They have bridged the generation gap by introducing things like a rock group at the eleven o'clock service and what they call rap sessions on subjects like drugs and sex instead of Sunday school. At the same time they admit privately that though the kids have a lot going for them, they wish they'd cut their hair properly. They're big on things like civil rights, peace, and the environment. They send their children to private school. They make people feel comfortable in their presence by showing them that they've got their feet on the ground like everybody else. They reassure them that religion is something you should take seriously but not go overboard with. (*See also* JOKE.)

2. Ministers have their heads in the clouds, which is just where you should have it when your mind is on higher things. Their morals are unimpeachable, and if you should ever happen to use bad language in their presence, you apologize. They have a lovely sense of humor and get a kick out of it every time you ask if they can't do something about all this rainy weather we've been having. They keep things like sex, politics, race, and alcoholism out of their sermons. Their specialty is religion, and they're wise enough to leave other matters to people who know what they're talking about.

3. Ministers are as anachronistic as alchemists or chimney sweeps. Like Tiffany glass or the Queen of England, their function is primarily decorative. Although their various

perspectives are admittedly limited, rapists and rape victims, drug addicts, victims and perpetrators of child abuse and the like are all to be listened to for their special insights. The perspective of ministers, on the other hand, is so hopelessly distorted and biased that there is no point in listening to them unless you happen to share it.

The first ministers were the twelve disciples. There is no evidence that Jesus chose them because they were brighter or nicer than other people. In fact the New Testament record suggests that they were continually missing the point, jockeying for position, and when the chips were down, interested in nothing so much as saving their own skins. Their sole qualification seems to have been their initial willingness to rise to their feet when Jesus said, "Follow me." As Saint Paul put it later, "God chose what is foolish in the world to shame the wise, God chose what is weak in the world to shame the strong" (1 Corinthians 1:27).

When Jesus sent the twelve out into the world, his instructions were simple. He told them to preach the kingdom of God and to heal (Luke 9:2), with the implication that to do either right was in effect to do both (*see* HEALING). Fortunately for the world in general and the church in particular, the ability to do them is not dependent on either moral character or I.Q. To do them in the name of Christ is to be a minister. In the name of Christ not to do them is to be a bad joke. (*See also* REVEREND.)

MIRACLE

A cancer inexplicably cured. A voice in a dream. A statue that weeps. A miracle is an event that strengthens faith. It is possible to look at most miracles and find a rational explanation in terms of natural cause and effect. It is possible to look at Rembrandt's *Supper at Emmaus* and find a rational explanation in terms of paint and canvas.

Faith in God is less apt to proceed from miracles than miracles from faith in God. (*See also* HEALING.)

MORALITY

It is no secret that ideas about what is Right and what is Wrong vary from time to time and place to place. King Solomon would not be apt to see eye to eye with a Presbyterian missionary on the subject of monogamy. For that reason, a popular argument runs, morality is all relative to the tastes of the time and not to be taken any more seriously by the enlightened than tastes in food, dress, architecture, or anything else. At a certain level, this is indisputably so. But there is another level.

In order to be healthy, there are certain rules you can break only at your peril. Eat sensibly, get enough sleep and exercise, avoid bottles marked poison, don't jump out of boats unless you can swim, and so on.

In order to be happy, there are also certain rules you can break only at your peril. Be at peace with your neighbor, get rid of hatred and envy, tell the truth, avoid temptations to evil you're not strong enough to resist, don't murder, steal, and so on.

Both sets of rules are as valid for a third-century Hottentot as for a twentieth-century Norwegian, for a Muslim as for a Methodist bishop, for the Emperor Constantine as for Jackie Onassis.

Both sets of rules—the moral as well as the hygienic—describe not the way people feel life ought to be but the way they have found life is. (*See also* LAW.)

MUSIC

Whereas painters work with space—the croquet players on the lawn, behind them the dark foliage of the hedge, above them the sky—musicians work with time as one note follows another note the way tock follows tick.

Music both asks us and also enables us to listen to certain qualities of time—to the grandeur of time, says Bach, to the poignance of time, says Mozart, to the swing and shimmer of time, says Debussy, or however else you choose to put into words the richness and complexity of what each of them is wordlessly "saying."

We learn from music how to listen to the music of our own time—one moment of our lives following another moment the way the violin passage follows the flute, the way the sound of footsteps on the gravel follows the rustle of leaves in the wind which follows the barking of a dog almost too far away to hear.

Music helps us to "keep time" in the sense of keeping us in touch with time, not just time as an ever-flowing stream that bears all of us away at last but time also as a stream that every once in a while slows down and becomes transparent enough for us to see down to the stream bed the way at a wedding, say, or watching the sun rise, past, present, future are so caught up in a single moment that we catch a glimpse of the mystery that at its deepest place time is timeless.

MYSTERY

There are mysteries which you can solve by taking thought. For instance, a murder mystery whose mysteriousness must be dispelled in order for the truth to be known.

There are other mysteries which do not conceal a truth to think your way to but whose truth is itself the mystery. The mystery of your self, for example. The more you try to fathom it, the more fathomless it is revealed to be. No matter how much of your self you are able to objectify and examine, the quintessential, living part of yourself will always elude you, i.e., the part that is conducting the examination. Thus you do not solve the mystery, you live the mystery. And you do that not by fully knowing yourself but by fully being yourself.

To say that God is a mystery is to say that you can never nail him down. Even on Christ the nails proved ultimately ineffective.

MYSTICISM

Mysticism is where religions start. Moses with his flocks in Midian, Buddha under the Bo tree, Jesus up to his knees in the waters of Jordan, each of them is responding to Something of which words like *Shalom, Nirvana, God* even, are only pallid souvenirs. Religion as ethics, institution, dogma, ritual, Scripture, social action, all of this comes later and in the long run maybe counts for less. Religions start, as Frost said poems do, with a lump in the throat—to put it mildly—or with a bush going up in flames, a rain of flowers, a dove coming down out of the sky. "I have seen things," Aquinas told a friend, "that make all my writings seem like straw."

Most people have also seen such things. Through some moment of beauty or pain, some sudden turning of their lives, most of them have caught glimmers at least of what the saints are blinded by. Only then, unlike the saints, they tend to go on as though nothing has happened.

We are all more mystics than we choose to let on, even to ourselves. Life is complicated enough as it is.

MYTH

The raw material of a myth, like the raw material of a dream, may be something that actually happened once. But myths, like dreams, do not tell us much about that kind of actuality. The creation of Adam and Eve, the Tower of Babel, Oedipus—they do not tell us primarily about events. They tell us about ourselves.

In popular usage, a myth has come to mean a story that is not true. Historically speaking, that may well be so. Humanly speaking, a myth is a story that is always true.

Nn

NAME (*See* BUECHNER, YHWH)

NEIGHBOR

When Jesus said to love your neighbor, a lawyer who was present asked him to clarify what he meant by *neighbor.* He wanted a legal definition he could refer to in case the question of loving one ever happened to come up. He presumably wanted something on the order of: "A neighbor (hereinafter referred to as the party of the first part) is to be construed as meaning a person of Jewish descent whose legal residence is within a radius of no more than three statute miles from one's own legal residence unless there is another person of Jewish descent (hereinafter to be referred to as the party of the second part) living closer to the party of the first part than one is oneself, in which case the party of the second part is to be construed as neighbor to the party of the first part and one is oneself relieved of all responsibility of any sort or kind whatsoever."

Instead Jesus told the story of the Good Samaritan (Luke 10:25–37), the point of which seems to be that your neighbor is to be construed as meaning anybody who needs you. The lawyer's response is left unrecorded. (*See also* LOVE.)

Oo

OBEDIENCE (*See* FREEDOM)

OMNIPRESENCE (*See* UBIQUITY)

OMNISCIENCE (*See* PREDESTINATION)

ORIGINAL SIN (*See* SIN)

Pp

PACIFISM (*See* PRINCIPLES)

PARABLE

A parable is a small story with a large point. Most of the ones Jesus told have a kind of sad fun about them. The parables of the Crooked Judge (Luke 18:1–8), the Sleepy Friend (Luke 11:5–8), and the Distraught Father (Luke 11:11–13) are really jokes in their way, at least part of whose point seems to be that a silly question deserves a silly answer. (*See also* PRAYER.) In the Prodigal Son (Luke 15:11–32), the elder brother's pious pique when the returning prodigal gets the red-carpet treatment is worthy of Molière's *Tartuffe,* as is the outraged legalism of the Laborers in the Vineyard (Matthew 20:1–16) when Johnny-Come-Lately gets as big a slice of the worm as the Early Bird. The point of the Unjust Steward is that it's better to be a resourceful rascal than a saintly schlemiel (Luke 16:1–8); and of the Talents that, spiritually speaking, playing the market will get you further than playing it safe (Matthew 25:14–30).

Both the sadness and the fun are at their richest, however, in the parable of the Great Banquet (Luke 14:16–24). The Beautiful People all send in their excuses, of course—their real estate, their livestock, their sex lives—so the host sends his social secretary out into the streets to bring in the poor, the maimed, the blind, the lame.

The string ensemble strikes up the overture to *The Bartered Bride,* the champagne glasses are filled, the cold pheasant is passed round, and there they sit by candlelight with their white canes and their empty sleeves, their Youngstown haircuts, their orthopedic shoes, their sleazy clothes, their aluminum walkers. A woman with a harelip proposes a toast. An old man with the face of Lear on the heath and a party hat does his best to rise to his feet. A deaf-mute thinks people are starting to go home and pushes back from the table. Rose petals float in the finger bowls. The strings shift into the *Liebestod.*

With parables and jokes both, if you've got to have it explained, don't bother.

PARENTS

"Honor your father and your mother," says the Fifth Commandment (Exodus 20:12). Honor them for having taken care of you before you were old enough to take care of yourself. Honor them for the sacrifices they made on your behalf, including the ones you would have kept them from making if you'd had the chance. Honor them for having loved you.

But how do you honor them when, well-intentioned as they may have been, they made terrible mistakes with you that have shadowed your life ever since? How do you honor them when, far from loving you or taking care of you, they literally or otherwise abandoned you? How do you honor them when physically or sexually or emotionally they abused you?

The answer seems to be that you are to honor them even so. Honor them for the pain that made them what they were and kept them from being what they might otherwise have become. Honor them because there were times when, even at their worst, they were doing the best they knew how to do. Honor them for the roles they were appointed to play—Father and Mother—because even when they played them abominably or didn't play them at all, the roles themselves are holy the way priesthood is holy even when the priest is a scoundrel. Honor them because, however unthinkingly or irresponsibly, they gave you your life.

PAUL

Paul's mads were madder and his blues bluer, his pride prouder and his humbleness humbler, his strengths stronger and his weaknesses weaker than almost anybody else's you'd be apt to think of; and the splash he made when he fell for Christ is audible still. It is little wonder that from the start he was a genius at making enemies.

As his own letters indicate, his contemporaries accused him of being insincere, crooked, yellow, physically repulsive, unclean, bumbling, and off his rocker. Since then the charges against him have tended to narrow down to one, i.e., that he took the simple and beautiful Gospel of Jesus and loused it up with obscure, divisive, and unnecessary theological subtleties.

Anybody who thinks the Gospel of Jesus is simple should go back and take a look at it. *Love your neighbor, Be ye perfect, Resist not evil, I and the Father are one, Follow me*—the only thing that's simple about the Gospel is the language.

How? Why? Whence? Whither? These are the questions Paul digs into with all the gentleness and tact of a pneumatic drill. Jesus exploded on the scene like a bomb and blew the world in general and the world of Judaism in particular sky-high. It was left to Paul to try to sort out the pieces.

He wrote the church at Corinth what he got for his pains: "Five times I have received at the hands of the Jews the forty lashes less one. Three times I have been beaten with rods. Once I was stoned. Three times I have been shipwrecked. A night and a day I have been adrift at sea. In danger from rivers . . . robbers . . . my own people . . . Gentiles. In toil and hardship, through many a sleepless night, in hunger and thirst . . . in cold and exposure . . ." (2 Corinthians 11:24–27). One hears the whines and boasts of Shylock. One wishes he hadn't been the one who had to say it. But he says it and means it.

And then he says, "I will not boast except of my weakness," and he means that too. The God who could work through the likes of him, he says, must be a God and a half.

So with a cauliflower ear and a split lip and whatever he meant by the thorn in the flesh that God gave "to keep me from being too elated" (2 Corinthians 12:7), he went his way and wrote his marvelous punch-drunk, Christ-drunk letters. Jesus lit the fire, and Paul used it to forge for him a church.

For some account of his conversion and how he tried to interpret it, *see* JUSTIFICATION, SANCTIFICATION, ETERNAL LIFE.

PEACE

Peace has come to mean the time when there aren't any wars or even when there aren't any major wars. Beggars can't be choosers; we'd most of us settle for that. But in Hebrew peace, *shalom,* means fullness, means having everything you need to be wholly and happily yourself.

One of the titles by which Jesus is known is Prince of Peace, and he used the word himself in what seem at first glance to be two radically contradictory utterances. On one occasion he said to the disciples, "Do not think that I have come to bring peace on earth; I have not come to bring peace, but a sword" (Matthew 10:34). And later on, the last time they ate together, he said to them, "Peace I leave with you; my peace I give to you" (John 14:27).

The contradiction is resolved when you realize that for Jesus peace seems to have meant not the absence of struggle, but the presence of love.

PHYSICIAN

We go to him with whatever ails us. We take off what the nurse asks us to and sit there until he appears. Who knows what the examination will reveal, but we try to prepare ourselves for the worst. It is not just our bodies that we are putting on the line but maybe even our chance for survival.

We are no longer in control of our future but like children can only wait for a grown-up to determine it. Stripped of our dignity and self-confidence no less than of most of our clothes, we perhaps don't feel quite so vulnerable anywhere else on earth.

When the physician finally steps through the door and starts checking us over, we hang not just on every word he speaks but on the look in his eyes and the tone of his voice for some clue to what he makes of us. When he finally tells us, we listen as though our lives depend on it, which quite possibly they do. If he knows his business, in just the touch of his hands there is healing.

Several times in the Gospels, Jesus indirectly refers to himself as a physician (Matthew 9:12, Luke 4:23, etc.). It is a richly touching and suggestive image.

POVERTY

In a sense we are all hungry and in need, but most of us don't recognize it. With plenty to eat in the deep freeze, with a roof over our heads and a car in the garage, we assume that the empty feeling inside must be just a case of the blues that can be cured by a Florida vacation, a new TV, an extra drink before supper.

The poor, on the other hand, are under no such delusion. When Jesus says, "Come unto me all ye who labor and are heavy laden, and I will give you rest" (Matthew 11:28), the poor stand a better chance than most of knowing what he's talking about and knowing that he's talking to them. In desperation they may even be willing to consider the possibility of accepting his offer. This is perhaps why Jesus on several occasions called them peculiarly blessed. (*See also* RICHES.)

PRAISE

You praise the heartbreaking beauty of Jessye Norman singing the *Vier Letzte Lieder* of Richard Strauss. You praise the new puppy for making its offering on the lawn for once instead of on the living-room rug. Maybe you yourself are praised for some generous thing you have done. In each case, the praise that is handed out is a measured response. It is a matter of saying something to one degree or another complimentary, with the implication that if Jessye Norman's voice had sprung a leak or the puppy hadn't made it outside in time or your generous deed turned out to be secretly self-serving, a different sort of response altogether would have been called for.

The way the 148th Psalm describes it, praising God is another kettle of fish altogether. It is about as measured as a volcanic eruption, and there is no implication that under any conceivable circumstances it could be anything other than what it is. The whole of creation is in on the act—the sun and moon, the sea, fire and snow, Holstein cows and white-throated sparrows, old men in walkers and children who still haven't taken their first step. Their praise is not chiefly a matter of *saying* anything because most of creation doesn't deal in words. Instead the snow whirls, the fire roars, the Holstein bellows, the old man watches the moon rise. Their praise is not something that at their most complimentary they say but something that at their truest they are.

We learn to praise God not by paying compliments but by paying attention. Watch how the trees exult when the wind is in them. Mark the utter stillness of the great blue heron in the swamp. Listen to the sound of the rain. Learn how to say *Hallelujah* from the ones who say it right.

PRAYER

We all pray whether we think of it as praying or not. The odd silence we fall into when something very beautiful is happening, or something very good or very bad. The ah-h-h-h! that sometimes floats up out of us as out of a Fourth of July crowd when the skyrocket bursts over the water. The stammer of pain at somebody else's pain. The stammer of joy at somebody else's joy. Whatever words or sounds we use for sighing with over our own lives. These are all prayers in their way. These are all spoken not just to ourselves but to something even more familiar than ourselves and even more strange than the world.

According to Jesus, by far the most important thing about praying is to keep at it. The images he uses to explain this are all rather comic, as though he thought it was rather comic to have to explain it at all. He says God is like a friend you go to borrow bread from at midnight. The friend tells you in effect to drop dead, but you go on knocking anyway until finally he gives you what you want so he can go back to bed again (Luke 11:5–8). Or God is like a crooked judge who refuses to hear the case of a certain poor widow, presumably because he knows there's nothing much in it for him. But she keeps on hounding him until finally he hears her case just to get her out of his hair (Luke 18:1–8). Even a stinker, Jesus says, won't give his own child a black eye when the child asks for peanut butter and jelly, so how all the more will God when *his* children . . . (Matthew 7:9–11)?

Be importunate, Jesus says—not, one assumes, because you have to beat a path to God's door before he'll open it, but because until you beat the path maybe there's no way of getting to *your* door. "Ravish my heart," John Donne wrote. But God will not usually ravish. He will only court.

Whatever else it may or may not be, prayer is at least talking to yourself, and that's in itself not always a bad idea.

Talk to yourself about your own life, about what you've done and what you've failed to do, and about who you are and who you wish you were and who the people you love are and the people you don't love too. Talk to yourself about what matters most to you, because if you don't, you may forget what matters most to you.

Even if you don't believe anybody's listening, at least you'll be listening.

Believe Somebody is listening. Believe in miracles. That's what Jesus told the father who asked him to heal his epileptic son. Jesus said, "All things are possible to him who believes." And the father spoke for all of us when he answered, "Lord, I believe; help my unbelief!" (Mark 9:14–29).

What about when the boy is not healed? When, listened to or not listened to, the prayer goes unanswered? Who knows? Just keep praying, Jesus says. Remember the sleepy friend, the crooked judge. Even if the boy dies, keep on beating the path to God's door, because the one thing you can be sure of is that down the path you beat with even your most half-cocked and halting prayer the God you call upon will finally come, and even if he does not bring you the answer you want, he will bring you himself. And maybe at the secret heart of all our prayers that is what we are really praying for. (*See also* JOB, HEALING.)

PREDESTINATION

It is the theory that since God knows everything else, he must also know whether each one of us is going to end up in Heaven or in Hell, and therefore the die is cast before we even cast it.

Theorizing about God this way is like an isosceles triangle trying to theorize the Great Pyramid of Cheops into the two dimensions of the printed page.

The fact that I know you so well that I know what you're going to do before you do it does not mean that you are not free to do whatever you damn well please.

"Logic" is only "cigol" spelled backward.

PRIDE

Pride is self-love, and in that sense a Christian is enjoined to be proud, i.e., another way of saying "Love your neighbor as yourself" is to say, "Love yourself as your neighbor." That doesn't mean your pulse is supposed to quicken every time you look in the mirror any more than it's supposed to quicken every time your neighbor passes the window. It means simply that the ability to work for your own good despite all the less than admirable things you know about yourself is closely related to the ability to work for your neighbors' good despite all the less than admirable things you know about them. It also means that just as in this sense love of self and love of neighbor go hand in hand, so do dislike of self and dislike of neighbor. For example: (a) the more I dislike my neighbors, the more I'm apt to dislike myself for disliking them, and them for making me dislike myself, and so on; and (b) I am continually tempted to take out on my neighbors the dislike I feel for myself, just the way if I crack my head on a low door I'm very apt to kick the first cat, child, or chair unlucky enough to catch my bloodshot eye.

Self-love or pride is a sin when, instead of leading you to share with others the self you love, it leads you to keep your self in perpetual safe-deposit. You not only don't accrue any interest that way, but become less and less interesting every day. (*See also* HUMILITY.)

PRINCIPLES

Principles are what people have instead of God.

To be a Christian means among other things to be willing if necessary to sacrifice even your highest principles for God's or your neighbor's sake the way a Christian pacifist must be willing to pick up a baseball bat if there's no other way to stop a man from savagely beating a child.

Jesus didn't forgive his executioners on principle but because in some unimaginable way he was able to love them.

"Principle" is an even duller word than "religion." (*See also* IDOLATRY.)

PROPHET

Prophet means *spokesman,* not *fortune-teller.* The one whom in their unfathomable audacity the prophets claimed to speak for was the Lord and Creator of the universe. There is no evidence to suggest that anyone ever asked a prophet home for supper more than once.

One day some city boys followed along behind the Prophet Elisha calling him "Bald-head!" Elisha summoned two she-bears, who tore forty-two of the city boys limb from limb. He then continued on his way to keep an appointment at Mount Carmel (2 Kings 2:23–25).

The Prophet Jeremiah showed a clay pot to a crowd of Judeans and told them it represented Judah. Then he smashed it to smithereens and told them that this was an expurgated version of what God had in mind to do to them (Jeremiah 19). He was right.

In a dream, the Prophet Ezekiel ate a copy of the Bible, thumb index and all, to show how sweet as honey was the word of God (Ezekiel 3:1–3).

In the time of the Prophet Amos, the Israelites looked forward eagerly to the day when the Lord would finally come and deliver them from all their afflictions. Amos told them they had better start looking forward to something else because when the day came, the Lord was going to settle a lot of people's hash all right, but the hash that would be settled first was Israel's. Quoting God, Amos went on to say, "Your great cathedrals bore me just as stiff as your TV evangelists, and your prayer breakfasts at the White House cause me no less abdominal discomfort than your dashboard Virgins. *Justice* is what I want, not photo opportunities, and *righteousness* like an ever-flowing stream" (Amos 5:21–24). Jeremiah was thrown into a cistern, and the rumor is that Isaiah was sawed in half. It is not recorded how Amos got his.

When the unknown prophet who wrote the last chapters of Isaiah pondered the question, What were the Chosen People chosen *for*? his answer was that they were chosen not to overwhelm the world in triumph but to suffer and die for the world in love. One thinks of the gas ovens of Auschwitz and of Anne Frank. One thinks of the anti-Semitic joke and the

Restricted Neighborhood. One also thinks of Jesus of Nazareth, who, when he went back to his hometown, chose this prophet to read from in the local synagogue (Luke 4:16–19). It is the words of this prophet that perhaps describe Jesus best—"a man of sorrows, and acquainted with grief" (Isaiah 53:3). *Acquainted* with grief. The way Jesus described his mission in the world was "to give his life as a ransom for many" (Mark 10:45).

The prophets were drunk on God, and in the presence of their terrible tipsiness, no one was ever comfortable. With a total lack of tact, they roared out against phoniness and corruption wherever they found them. They were the terror of kings and priests. The Prophet Nathan tells King David to his face that he is a crook and an adulterer (2 Samuel 12:1–15). The Prophet Jeremiah goes straight to the Temple itself and says, "Do not trust in these deceptive words, 'This is the Temple of the Lord, the Temple of the Lord, the Temple of the Lord' " (Jeremiah 7:4). It was like a prophet to say it three times, just to make sure.

No prophet is on record as having asked for the job. When God put the finger on Isaiah, Isaiah said, "How long, O Lord?" (Isaiah 6:11) and couldn't have been exactly reassured by the answer he was given. Jeremiah pled that he was much too young for that type of work (Jeremiah 1:6). Moses sounded like a prophet when he pointed out to God that he'd never been much good at public speaking and the chances were that Pharaoh wasn't going to give him so much as the time of day (Exodus 4:1–13). Like Abraham Lincoln's story about the man being ridden out of town on a rail, if it wasn't for the honor of the thing, the prophets would all have rather walked.

Most of the prophets went a little mad before they were through, if they weren't a little mad to begin with. Ezekiel kept seeing wheels with eyes around the rims. John the Baptist ate bugs. You can hardly blame them.

Karl Marx, Friedrich Nietzsche, Jonathan Swift, and Malcolm X were all prophets in their ways. So was Ayn Rand. So are Gloria Steinem and Rosa Parks.

Like Robert Frost's, a prophet's quarrel with the world is deep-down a lover's quarrel. If they didn't love the world, they probably wouldn't bother to tell it that it's going to Hell. They'd just let it go. Their quarrel is God's quarrel.

PURGATORY

According to Roman Catholic doctrine, some people go to Heaven when they die, some people go to Hell, and some people, although they will get to Heaven eventually, have to make a preliminary detour through Purgatory, where the sins that still cling to them are purged away through suffering. Protestants reject this notion partly because of the unpleasant odor it developed during the Middle Ages, when if you put so much cash on the line, the church guaranteed to arrange at least a substantial reduction in your Purgatorial sentence, and partly because of the general Protestant view that when you are saved by God, that means among other things that you are saved from torment, however edifying, after death.

What is persuasive about the Catholic view is the implication that even with God on their side people do not attain to what Saint Paul calls "mature manhood, the measure of the stature of the fullness of Christ" (Ephesians 4:13) overnight. At best the job is unlikely to be more than the slimmest fraction done by the time they die.

An Anglican prayer for someone who has died includes the words "grant that, increasing in knowledge and love of thee, he may go from strength to strength, in the life of perfect service, in thy heavenly kingdom." Increasing in knowledge. From strength to strength. Whichever side of the grave you are talking about, life with God apparently involves growth and growing pains.

The sacrament of bread and wine administered to the dying is known as the *viaticum*, which means provision for a journey or one for the road. Whether or not you think of it in connection with Purgatory, *viaticum* suggests that many a high adventure still awaits you and many a cobbled street before you finally reach the fountain in the square.

Qq

QUESTIONS

On her deathbed, Gertrude Stein is said to have asked, "What is the answer?" Then, after a long silence, "What is the question?" Don't start looking in the Bible for the answers it gives. Start by listening for the questions it asks.

We are much involved, all of us, with questions about things that matter a good deal today but will be forgotten by this time tomorrow—the immediate wheres and whens and hows that face us daily at home and at work—but at the same time we tend to lose track of the questions about things that matter always, life-and-death questions about meaning, purpose, and value. To lose track of such deep questions as these is to risk losing track of who we really are in our own depths and where we are really going. There is perhaps no stronger reason for reading the Bible than that somewhere among all those India-paper pages there awaits each man and woman, whoever they are, the one question which (though for years they may have been pretending not to hear it) is the central question of his or her own life. Here are a few of them:

- What is a man profited if he shall gain the whole world and lose his own soul? (Matthew 16:26)
- Am I my brother's keeper? (Genesis 4:9)
- If God is for us, who can be against us? (Romans 8:31)
- What is truth? (John 18:38)
- How can a man be born when he is old? (John 3:4)

- What does a man gain by all the toil at which he toils under the sun? (Ecclesiastes 1:3)
- Whither shall I go from thy Spirit? (Psalm 139:7)
- Who is my neighbor? (Luke 10:29)
- What shall I do to inherit eternal life? (Luke 10:25)

When you hear the question that is your question, then you have already begun to hear much. Whether you can accept the Bible's answer or not, you have reached the point where at least you can begin to hear it too.

Rr

REASON (*See* REVELATION)

RELIGION

The word *religion* points to that area of human experience where one way or another we come upon Mystery as a summons to pilgrimage; where we sense beyond and beneath the realities of every day a Reality no less real because it can only be hinted at in myths and rituals; where we glimpse a destination that we can never fully know until we reach it.

Since the Reality that religion claims to deal with is beyond space and time, we cannot use normal space-and-time language (i.e., nouns and verbs) to describe it directly. We must fall back on the language of metaphor and resign ourselves to describing it at best indirectly.

It is obvious that this is what we are doing when we say Jesus is "the son of God," or the Lord is our "shepherd," or the kingdom of God is "within you." It is not so obvious that this is what we are doing—but we are doing it no less—when we say, "God exists." This does not mean that God "exists" literally as you and I do—i.e., exists now and not then, here and not there, and stands out of (*ex* + *sistere*) some prior reality. It is at best a crude metaphor.

To say that God "does not exist" may be a better metaphor to suggest the nature of God's reality. But since it also is bound to be taken literally, it is better not to say it.

RELIGIOUS BOOKS

There are *poetry* books and *poetic* books—the first a book with poems in it, the second a book which may or may not have poems in it but which is in some sense a poem itself.

In much the same way there are *religion* books and *religious* books. A *religion* book is a book with religion in it in the everyday sense of religious ideas, symbols, attitudes, and—if it takes the form of fiction—with characters and settings that have overtly religious associations and implications. There are good religion books like *The Scarlet Letter* by Hawthorne or *Wise Blood* by Flannery O'Connor, and there are miserable ones like most of what is called "Christian" fiction.

A *religious* book may not have any religion as such in it at all, but to read it is in some measure to experience firsthand what a *religion* book can only tell about. A *religion* book is a canvas. A *religious* book is a transparency. With a *religious* book it is less what we see in it than what we see through it that matters. John Irving's *A Prayer for Owen Meany* would be an example. *Huckleberry Finn* would be another.

Writers of *religious* books tend to achieve most when they are least conscious of doing so. The attempt to be religious is as doomed as the attempt to be poetic. Thus in the writing, as in the reading, a *religious* book is an act of grace—no less rare, no less precious, no less improbable.

REPENTANCE

To repent is to come to your senses. It is not so much something you do as something that happens. True repentance spends less time looking at the past and saying, "I'm sorry," than to the future and saying, "Wow!"

RESURRECTION (*See* IMMORTALITY)

REVELATION

There are two different ways of describing how you came to know something. One way is to say *you found it out*. The other way is to say *it occurred to you*. Reason is involved in both. To say you *found out* that So-and-So was the best friend you had suggests that you reasoned your way to such a conclusion. To say it *occurred to you* suggests that although the conclusion was not reached by reason, it was not incompatible with it.

It occurred to you as distinct from *you found out* suggests knowledge given as distinct from knowledge earned. It suggests inner meaning as distinct from outer semblance. For example, I *found out* that Francis of Assisi gave all his money to the poor, called the sun his brother, and preached sermons to birds. But *it occurred to me* that he must be a saint. Or an idiot.

Revelation means knowledge as grace. Nobody has ever managed to *find out* much if anything about God (*see* THEOLOGY).

Classic Buddhism is reasonable, *found out*, and doesn't claim to be otherwise. In the Four Noble Truths, Buddha puts it in a nutshell. Like the family doctor, he diagnoses our ailment and prescribes a cure. He says (1) that the name of our ailment is Life, which causes great pain because we know that it always falls to pieces in the end. He says (2) that if we didn't like Life so much, we wouldn't mind having it fall to pieces in the end. Therefore, he says, (3) the way to get cured of the ailment is to stop clinging to Life as though it were a prize instead of a pain in the neck. Finally (4) he outlines eight steps for getting out of Life and into Nirvana.

Classic Christianity, on the other hand, is not primarily reasonable or something we have *found out* or worked out for ourselves. Christ came. He healed people. He forgave people their sins and said to love everybody including your enemy. He died in a peculiarly unpleasant way, forgiving his executioners. Christianity was born when *it occurred* to some of the ones who had known him that his kind of life was the only kind worth living, and that in some invisible way Christ was still around to help them live it.

Nobody figured Christianity out. It happened. That is what it means to call it a *revealed* religion—not incompatible with reason maybe, if you give it some thought, but not arrived at primarily by reason either.

REVEREND

A title of respect to be used only in the third person, if then. Speak *about* the Reverend Susan Smith if you have to, but never go up to her and say, "That's telling them, Reverend!" any more than you'd go up to a Senator and say, "How are things in Washington, Honorable?"

Reverend means *to be revered.* Ministers are not to be revered for who they are in themselves, but for who it is they represent, just as the Spanish Ambassador is seated at the hostess's right not because of his *beaux yeux* but because he represents the King. (*See also* MINISTER.)

RICHES

The trouble with being rich is that since you can solve with your checkbook virtually all of the practical problems that bedevil ordinary people, you are left in your leisure with nothing but the great human problems to contend with: how to be happy, how to love and be loved, how to find meaning and purpose in your life.

In desperation the rich are continually tempted to believe that they can solve these problems too with their checkbooks, which is presumably what led Jesus to remark one day that for a rich man to get to Heaven is about as easy as for a Cadillac to get through a revolving door.

RIGHTEOUSNESS

"You haven't got it *right!*" says the exasperated piano teacher. Junior is holding his hands the way he's been told. His fingering is unexceptionable. He has memorized the piece perfectly. He has hit all the proper notes with deadly accuracy. But his heart's not in it, only his fingers. What he's playing is a sort of music but nothing that will start voices singing or feet tapping. He has succeeded in boring everybody to death including himself.

Jesus said to his disciples, "Unless your righteousness exceeds that of the scribes and Pharisees, you will never enter the kingdom of Heaven" (Matthew 5:20). The scribes and Pharisees were playing it by the Book. They didn't slip up on a single do or don't. But they were getting it all wrong.

Righteousness is getting it all *right.* If you play it the way it's supposed to be played, there shouldn't be a still foot in the house.

RITUAL

A wedding. A handshake. A kiss. A coronation. A parade. A dance. A meal. A graduation. A ritual is the ceremonial acting out of the profane in order to show forth its sacredness. A sacrament (q.v.) is the breaking through of the sacred into the profane.

A sacrament is God offering his holiness to us. A ritual is our raising up the holiness of our humanity to God.

Ss

SABBATH

For Jews it is the seventh day, Saturday, and for most Christians it is the first day, Sunday. In either case, it is a day set aside from the other six as the day which God himself blessed and hallowed "because on it God rested from all his work which he had done in creation" (Genesis 2:3).

Banks and post offices are closed, and most businesses shut down. In some states you can't buy a drink, and the regular weekday newscasters are replaced by substitutes. Religiously inclined people may go to church. Otherwise life goes on much as always. The shopping malls are usually just as crowded as on any other day, many of the roads are even more so, and newspapers swell to grotesque proportions. Insofar as it is still treated as a day of rest, the rest is apt to consist of people knocking themselves out on tennis courts, golf courses, hiking trails, or doing things like mowing the lawn, painting the back porch, paying bills, or taking a long afternoon nap.

You think of God resting after the creation was finally all created. You think of the deep hush of it, like the hush between breakers at the beach. You think of the new creation itself resting—the grey squirrel ceasing to twitch and chatter, the kingfisher settling down on the branch by the pond, the man and the woman standing still in the garden. You think of God blessing this one day of the seven and hallowing it, making it holy.

The room is quiet. You're not feeling tired enough to sleep or energetic enough to go out. For the moment there is nowhere else you'd rather go, no one else you'd rather be. You feel at home in your body. You feel at peace in your mind. For no particular reason, you let the palms of your hands come together and close your eyes. Sometimes it is only when you happen to taste a crumb of it that you dimly realize what it is that you're so hungry for you can hardly bear it.

SACRAMENT

A sacrament is when something holy happens. It is transparent time, time which you can see through to something deep inside time. (*See also* MUSIC.)

Generally speaking, Protestants have two official sacraments (the Lord's Supper, Baptism) and Roman Catholics these two plus five others (Confirmation, Penance, Extreme Unction, Ordination, and Matrimony). In other words, at such milestone moments as seeing a baby baptized or being baptized yourself, confessing your sins, getting married, dying, you are apt to catch a glimpse of the almost unbearable preciousness and mystery of life.

Needless to say, church isn't the only place where the holy happens. Sacramental moments can occur at any moment, at any place, and to anybody. Watching something get born. Making love. A walk on the beach. Somebody coming to see you when you're sick. A meal with people you love. Looking into a stranger's eyes and finding out he's not a stranger.

If we weren't blind as bats, we might see that life itself is sacramental. (*See also* BAPTISM, LORD'S SUPPER, RITUAL.)

SACRIFICE

To sacrifice something is to majke it holy by giving it away for love.

SAINT

In his holy flirtation with the world, God occasionally drops a pocket handkerchief. These handkerchiefs are called saints.

Many people think of saints as plaster saints or moral exemplars, men and women of such paralyzing virtue that they never thought a nasty thought or did an evil deed their whole lives long. As far as I know, real saints never even come close to characterizing themselves that way. On the contrary, no less a saint than Saint Paul wrote to Timothy, "I am foremost among sinners" (1 Timothy 1:15), and Jesus himself prayed God to forgive him his trespasses, and when the rich young man addressed him as "good Teacher," answered, "No one is good but God alone" (Mark 10:18).

In other words, the feet of saints are as much of clay as everybody else's, and their sainthood consists less of what they have done than of what God has for some reason chosen to do through them. When you consider that Saint Mary Magdalen was possessed by seven devils, that Saint Augustine prayed, "Give me chastity and continence, but not now," that Saint Francis started out as a high-living young dude in downtown Assisi, and that Saint Simeon Stylites spent years on top of a sixty-foot pillar, you figure that maybe there's nobody God can't use as a means of grace including even ourselves.

The Holy Spirit has been called "the Lord, the giver of life," and drawing their power from that source, saints are essentially life-givers. To be with them is to become more alive.

SALVATION

It is an experience first and a doctrine second.

Doing the work you're best at doing and like to do best, hearing great music, having great fun, seeing something very beautiful, weeping at somebody else's tragedy—all these experiences are related to the experience of salvation because in all of them two things happen: (1) you lose yourself, and (2) you find that you are more fully yourself than usual.

A closer analogy is the experience of love. When you love somebody, it is no longer yourself who is the center of your own universe. It is the one you love who is. You forget yourself. You deny yourself. You give of yourself, so that by all the rules of arithmetical logic there should be less of yourself than there was to start with. Only by a curious paradox there is more. You feel that at last you really *are* yourself.

The experience of salvation involves the same paradox. Jesus put it like this: "He who loses his life for my sake will find it" (Matthew 10:39).

You give up your old self-seeking self for somebody you love and thereby become yourself at last. You must die with Christ so that you can rise with him, Paul says. It is what baptism (q.v.) is all about.

You do not love God so that, tit for tat, he will then save you. To love God is to be saved. To love anybody is a significant step along the way.

You do not love God and live for him so you will go to Heaven. Whichever side of the grave you happen to be talking about, to love God and live for him *is* Heaven.

It is a gift, not an achievement.

You can make yourself moral. You can make yourself religious. But you can't make yourself love.

"We love," John says, "because he first loved us" (1 John 4:19).

Who knows how the awareness of God's love first hits people. We all have our own tales to tell, including those of us who wouldn't believe in God if you paid us. Some moment happens in your life that you say Yes to right up to the roots of your hair, that makes it worth having been born just to have happen. Laughing with somebody till the tears run down your cheeks. Waking up to the first snow. Being in bed with somebody you love.

Whether you thank God for such a moment or thank your lucky stars, it is a moment that is trying to open up your whole life. If you turn your back on such a moment and hurry along to Business as Usual, it may lose you the ball game. If you throw your arms around such a moment and bless it, it may save your soul.

How about the person you know who as far as you can possibly tell has never had such a moment—the soreheads and slobs of the world, the ones the world has hopelessly crippled? Maybe for that person the moment that has to happen is you.

It is a process, not an event. (*See also* JUSTIFICATION, SANCTIFICATION, ETERNAL LIFE, SIN.)

SANCTIFICATION

In "Beauty and the Beast," it is only when the Beast discovers that Beauty really loves him in all his ugliness that he himself becomes beautiful.

In the experience of Saint Paul, it is only when we discover that God really loves us in all our unloveliness that we ourselves start to become godlike (*see* JUSTIFICATION).

Paul's word for this gradual transformation of a sow's ear into a silk purse is *sanctification,* and he sees it as the second stage in the process of salvation.

Being sanctified is a long and painful stage because with part of themselves sinners prefer their sin, just as with part of himself the Beast prefers his glistening snout and curved tusks. Many drop out with the job hardly more than begun, and among those who stay with it there are few if any who don't drag their feet most of the way.

But little by little—less by taking pains than by taking it easy—the forgiven person starts to become a forgiving person, the healed person to become a healing person, the loved person to become a loving person. God does most of it. The end of the process, Paul says, is eternal life (q.v.).

SCIENCE

Science is the investigation of the physical universe and its ways, and consists largely of weighing, measuring, and putting things in test tubes. To assume that this kind of investigation can unearth solutions to all our problems is a form of religious faith whose bankruptcy has only in recent years started to become apparent.

There is a tendency in many people to suspect that anything that can't be weighed, measured, or put in a test tube is either not real or not worth talking about. That is like a blind person's suspecting that anything that can't be smelled, tasted, touched, or heard is probably a figment of the imagination.

A scientist's views on such subjects as God, morality, life after death are apt to be about as enlightening as a theologian's views on the structure of the atom or the cause and cure of the common cold.

The conflict between science and religion, which reached its peak toward the end of the last century, is like the conflict between a podiatrist and a poet. One says that Susie Smith has fallen arches. The other says she walks in beauty like the night. In his own way each is speaking the truth. What is at issue is the kind of truth you're after.

SECRETS

We tend to think right away of dark secrets—things we did or failed to do that we have never managed to forgive ourselves for; fierce hungers that we have difficulty admitting even to ourselves; things that happened to us long ago too painful to speak of; doubts about our own worth as human beings, doubts about the people closest to us, about God if we believe in God; and fear—the fear of death, the fear of life.

But there are also happy secrets, the secrets we keep like treasure less because we don't want to share them with the world for fear of somehow tarnishing them than because they are so precious we have no way of sharing them adequately. The love we feel for certain people, some of them people we scarcely know, some of them people who do not suspect our love and wouldn't know how to respond to it if they did. The way our hearts leap at certain things which the chances are wouldn't make anybody else so much as turn a hair—the sound of a particular voice on the telephone, a dog-eared book we read as children, the first snow, the sight of an old man smoking his pipe on the porch as we drive by.

We are our secrets. They are the essence of what makes us ourselves. They are the rich loam out of which, for better or worse, grow the selves by which the world knows us. If we are ever to be free and whole, we must be free from their darkness and have their spell over us broken. If we are ever to see each other as we fully are, we must see by their light.

"Search me, O God, and know my heart!" cries out the great 139th Psalm, which is all about the hiding and baring of secrets. "Try me and know my thoughts . . . for darkness is as light to thee." Even our darkness.

It is the secret prayer of us all.

SELF **(*See* MYSTERY)**

SENSES

Taste an apple. Taste salt.

See the sunlight on the wall, the deer track in the snow.

Hear the luffing of the sail.

Smell the rose, the dead mouse behind the wainscoting, the child's hair.

Touch the hand that is touching your hand.

Although we have been taught better, it is easier to assume that nothing that lies beyond the reach of our five senses is entirely real than to acknowledge that what we know about reality through the five senses is roughly the equivalent of what an ant crawling across the front page of the *New York Times* knows about the state of the world.

SERMON

"Don't preach to me!" means "Don't bore me to death with your offensive platitudes." Respectable verbs don't get into that kind of trouble entirely by accident.

Sermons are like jokes; even the best ones are hard to remember. In both cases that may be just as well. Ideally the thing to remember is not the preachers' eloquence but the lump in your throat or the heart in your mouth or the thorn in your flesh that appeared as much in spite of what they said as because of it.

Paul said, "Woe to me if I do not preach the gospel!" (1 Corinthians 9:16). Jesus said, "Whoever causes one of these little ones who believe in me to sin, it would be better for him to have a great millstone fastened round his neck and to be drowned in the depth of the sea" (Matthew 18:6). People who preach sermons without realizing that they're heading straight for Scylla and Charybdis ought to try a safer and more productive line of work.

SEX

Contrary to Mrs. Grundy, sex is not sin. Contrary to Hugh Hefner, it's not salvation either. Like nitroglycerin, it can be used either to blow up bridges or heal hearts.

At its roots, the hunger for food is the hunger for survival. At its roots the hunger to know a person sexually is the hunger to know and be known by that person humanly. Food without nourishment doesn't fill the bill for long, and neither does sex without humanness.

Adultery, promiscuity either heterosexual or homosexual, masturbation—one appealing view is that anything goes as long as nobody gets hurt. The trouble is that human beings are so hopelessly psychosomatic in composition that whatever happens to the *soma* happens also to the *psyche,* and vice versa.

Who is to say who gets hurt and who doesn't get hurt, and how? Maybe the injuries are all internal. Maybe it will be years before the X-rays show up anything. Maybe the only person who gets hurt is you.

In practice Jesus was notoriously soft on sexual misbehavior. Some of his best friends were hustlers. He saved the woman taken in adultery from stoning. He didn't tell the woman at the well that she ought to marry the man she was living with. Possibly he found their fresh-faced sensualities closer to loving God and humanity than the thin-lipped pieties of the Pharisees. Certainly he shared the Old Testament view that the body in all its manifestations was basically good because a good God made it.

But he also had some hard words to say about lust (Matthew 5:27–28), and told the adulterous woman to go and sin no more. When the force of a person's sexuality is centrifugal, pushing farther and farther away as *psyches* the very ones being embraced as *somas,* this sexuality is of the Devil. When it is centripetal, it is of God. (*See also* SIN.)

SIN

The power of sin is centrifugal. When at work in a human life, it tends to push everything out toward the periphery. Bits and pieces go flying off until only the core is left. Eventually bits and pieces of the core itself go flying off until in the end nothing at all is left. "The wages of sin is death" is Saint Paul's way of saying the same thing.

Other people and (if you happen to believe in him) God or (if you happen not to) the World, Society, Nature—whatever you call the greater whole of which you're part—sin is whatever you do, or fail to do, that pushes them away, that widens the gap between you and them and also the gaps within your self.

For example, the sin of the Pharisee is not just (a) his holier-than-thou attitude which pushes other people away, but (b) his secret suspicion that his own holiness is deficient too, which pushes part of himself away, and (c) his possibly not-so-subconscious feeling that anybody who expects him to be all that holy must be a cosmic SOB, which pushes Guess Who away.

Sex is sinful to the degree that, instead of drawing you closer to other human beings in their humanness, it unites bodies but leaves the lives inside them hungrier and more alone than before.

Religion and unreligion are both sinful to the degree that they widen the gap between you and the people who don't share your views.

The word *charity* illustrates the insidiousness of sin. From meaning *a free and loving gift* it has come to mean *a demeaning handout*.

"Original Sin" means we all originate out of a sinful world which taints us from the word go. We all tend to make ourselves the center of the universe, pushing away centrifugally from that center everything that seems to impede its freewheeling. More even than hunger, poverty, or disease, it is what Jesus said he came to save the world from. (*See also* SALVATION.)

SLOTH

Sloth is not to be confused with laziness. Lazy people, people who sit around and watch the grass grow, may be people at peace. Their sun-drenched, bumblebee dreaming may be the prelude to action or itself an act well worth the acting.

Slothful people, on the other hand, may be very busy people. They are people who go through the motions, who fly on automatic pilot. Like somebody with a bad head cold, they have mostly lost their sense of taste and smell. They know something's wrong with them, but not wrong enough to do anything about. Other people come and go, but through glazed eyes they hardly notice them. They are letting things run their course. They are getting through their lives.

SOUL (*See* SPIRIT, HEALING, SEX)

SPIRIT

The word *spirit* has come to mean something pale and shapeless, like an unmade bed. School spirit, the American spirit, the Christmas spirit, the spirit of '76, the Holy Spirit—each of these points to something you know is supposed to get you to your feet cheering, but which you somehow can't rise to. The adjective *spiritual* has become downright offensive. If somebody recommends a person as spiritual you tend to avoid that person, and usually with good reason. *Inspiring* is even worse. *Inspirational* is worse still. Inspirational books are almost invariably for the birds.

Like its counterparts in Hebrew and Greek, the Latin word *spiritus* originally meant *breath* (as in expire, respiratory, and so on), and breath is what you have when you're alive and don't have when you're dead. Thus spirit = breath = life, the aliveness and power of your life, and to speak of your spirit (or soul) is to speak of the power of life that is in you. When your spirit is unusually strong, the life in you unusually alive, you can breathe it out into other lives, become literally in-spiring.

Spirit is highly contagious. When people are very excited, very happy, very sad, you can catch it from them as easily as measles or a yawn. You can catch it from what they say or from what they do or just from what happens to the air of a room when they enter it without saying or doing anything. Groups also have a spirit, as anybody can testify who has ever been caught up in the spirit of a football game, a political rally, or a lynch mob. Spirit can be good or bad, healing or destructive. Spirit can be transmitted across great distances of time and space. For better or worse, you can catch the spirit of people long dead (Saint Thérèse of Lisieux or the Marquis de Sade), of people whose faces you have never seen and whose languages you cannot speak.

God also has a spirit—is Spirit, says the Apostle John (4:24). Thus God is the power of the power of life itself, has breathed and continues to breathe himself into his creation. In-spires it. The spirit of God, Holy Spirit, Holy Ghost, is highly contagious. When Peter and his friends were caught up in it at Jerusalem on Pentecost, everybody thought they were drunk even though the sun wasn't yet over the yardarm (Acts 2). They were. (*See also* TRINITY.)

SUPERSTITION

Superstition is the suspicion that things are seldom what they seem and usually worse. Breaking a mirror foreshadows a graver misfortune than having to buy a new one. Inviting thirteen for dinner involves a greater risk than not having enough to go round. The superstitious person may be more nearly right in being wrong than the person who takes everything at face value. If a black cat crosses your path and all you see is a black cat, you need to have more than your eyes examined. What is crossing your path with four legs and a hoisted tail is the dark and inscrutable mystery of creation itself.

Tt

THEOLOGY

Theology is the study of God and his ways. For all we know, dung beetles may study us and our ways and call it humanology. If so, we would probably be more touched and amused than irritated. One hopes that God feels likewise.

TIME (*See* ETERNITY)

TOLERATION

Toleration is often just Indifference in disguise.

"It doesn't matter what religion you have as long as you have one" is apt to mean really, "I couldn't care less whether you have one or not."

If it means what it says, the question arises about a religion which demands, say, that firstborn children be fed to the crocodiles to ensure a good harvest. Somewhere lines have to be drawn. Sometimes it's not so easy to draw them.

Buddhism says, "Those who love a hundred have a hundred woes. Those who love ten have ten woes. Those who love one have one woe. Those who love none have no woe." Christianity says, "He who does not love remains in death" (1 John 3:14). The trouble is that each speaks a different kind of truth. If you choose for one as the truer and more profound of the two, then you choose against the other, granting it only a kind of proximate validity. Thus toleration must be limited in the interests of honesty.

It is sometimes argued that in our society the young should not be taught about Christianity. They should be taught about all religions. That is like saying they should be taught comparative linguistics before they have mastered English grammar.

It is sometimes argued that no religion of any kind should be taught in schools. The name of God should not be mentioned, prayers should not be prayed, religious holidays should not be observed—all of this to avoid in any way indoctrinating the young. This is itself, of course, the most powerful kind of indoctrination because it is the most subtle and for that reason the hardest for the young or anybody else to defend themselves against. Given no reason to believe that the issue of God has any importance at all, or even exists as an issue, how can anybody make an intelligent decision either for God or against him?

My wife went to a college in the fifties which was so tolerant religiously that it wouldn't allow an ordained minister to conduct an informal discussion group on the campus.

TRAVEL

Sometimes we travel to get away and see something of the world. Sometimes we travel just to get away from ourselves. Sometimes we travel to convince ourselves that we are Getting Someplace.

The author of the Epistle to the Hebrews lists a number of gadabouts like Noah and Abraham, Sarah and Jacob, and the footloose Israelites generally. He then makes the point that what they were really doing was "seeking a homeland," which they died without ever finding but never gave up seeking even so (Hebrews 11:14).

Maybe that is true of all of us. Maybe at the heart of all our traveling is the dream of someday, somehow, getting Home.

TRINITY

The much-maligned doctrine of the Trinity is an assertion that, appearances to the contrary notwithstanding, there is only one God.

Father, Son, and Holy Spirit mean that the mystery beyond us, the mystery among us, and the mystery within us are all the same mystery. Thus the Trinity is a way of saying something about us and the way we experience God.

The Trinity is also a way of saying something about God and the way he is within himself, i.e., God does not need the Creation in order to have something to love, because within himself love happens. In other words, the love God is is love not as a noun but as a verb. This verb is reflexive as well as transitive.

If the idea of God as both Three and One seems farfetched and obfuscating, look in the mirror someday.

There is (a) the interior life known only to yourself and those you choose to communicate it to (the Father). There is (b) the visible face, which in some measure reflects that inner life (the Son). And there is (c) the invisible power you have which enables you to communicate that interior life in such a way that others do not merely know *about* it, but know it in the sense of its becoming part of who they are (the Holy Spirit). Yet what you are looking at in the mirror is clearly and indivisibly the one and only you.

TRUTH

When Jesus says that he has come to bear witness to the truth, Pilate asks, "What is truth?" (John 18:38). Contrary to the traditional view that his question is cynical, it is possible that he asks it with a lump in his throat. Instead of Truth, Pilate has only expedience. His decision to throw Jesus to the wolves is expedient. Pilate views humankind as alone in the universe with nothing but its own courage and ingenuity to see it through. That is enough to choke up anybody.

Pilate asks What is truth? and for years there have been politicians, scientists, theologians, philosophers, poets, and so on to tell him. The sound they make is like the sound of crickets chirping.

Jesus doesn't answer Pilate's question. He just stands there. *Stands*, and stands *there*.

Uu

UBIQUITY

Every automobile bears on its license plate a number which represents the number of years that have elapsed since the birth of Christ. This is a powerful symbol of the ubiquity of God and the indifference of the human race.

UGLINESS

Whoever the Suffering Servant was—that mysterious figure whom Isaiah saw as destined somehow to save the world by suffering for it, and in terms of whom Jesus apparently saw himself—we know that his appearance was "marred beyond human semblance and his form beyond that of the sons of men" (Isaiah 52:14). "He had no comeliness that we should look at him, and no beauty that we should desire him," Isaiah continues, and presumably that was a large part of why "he was despised and rejected by men" (Isaiah 53:2b–3a).

You think of the grossly overweight woman struggling to get through the turnstile at the county fair, the acne-scarred teenager at the high school prom, the skeletal AIDS victim sitting on the New York sidewalk with a styrofoam begging cup between his ankles. They too, like the Servant, are men and women "of sorrow and acquainted with grief" (Isaiah 53:3b).

Who knows to what extent their ugliness has led them too to be despised and rejected and to despise and reject themselves? Who knows whether their acquaintance with grief will open their hearts also to the grieving of others or whether it will turn their hearts to stone? But for the sake of the one who bore it before they did, we are to honor them for the sanctity of their burden. For his sake, we are called to see their terrible beauty.

Vv

VIRGIN BIRTH

The earliest of the four Gospels makes no reference to it, and neither does Paul, who wrote earlier still. On later evidence, however, many Christians have made it an article of faith that it was the Holy Spirit rather than Joseph who got Mary pregnant. If you believe God was somehow in Christ, it shouldn't make much difference to you how he got there. If you don't believe, it should make less difference still. In either case, life is complicated enough without confusing theology and gynecology.

In one sense anyway, the doctrine of the Virgin Birth is demonstrably true. Whereas the villains of history can always be seen as the products of heredity and environment, the saints always seem to arrive under their own steam. Evil evolves. Holiness happens.

VOCATION

It comes from the Latin *vocare,* to call, and means the work a person is called to by God.

There are all different kinds of voices calling you to all different kinds of work, and the problem is to find out which is the voice of God rather than of Society, say, or the Superego, or Self-Interest.

By and large a good rule for finding out is this: The kind of work God usually calls you to is the kind of work (a) that you need most to do and (b) that the world most needs to have done. If you really get a kick out of your work, you've presumably met requirement (a), but if your work is writing cigarette ads, the chances are you've missed requirement (b). On the other hand, if your work is being a doctor in a leper colony, you have probably met requirement (b), but if most of the time you're bored and depressed by it, the chances are you have not only bypassed (a), but probably aren't helping your patients much either.

Neither the hair shirt nor the soft berth will do. The place God calls you to is the place where your deep gladness and the world's deep hunger meet.

Ww

WINE

Unfermented grape juice is a bland and pleasant drink, especially on a warm afternoon mixed half-and-half with ginger ale. It is a ghastly symbol of the life blood of Jesus Christ, especially when served in individual antiseptic, thimble-sized glasses.

Wine is booze, which means it is dangerous and drunk-making. It makes the timid brave and the reserved amorous. It loosens the tongue and breaks the ice, especially when served in a loving cup. It kills germs. As symbols go, it is a rather splendid one.

WISHFUL THINKING

Christianity is mainly wishful thinking. Even the part about Judgment and Hell reflects the wish that somewhere the score is being kept.

Dreams are wishful thinking. Children playing at being grown-up is wishful thinking. Interplanetary travel is wishful thinking.

Sometimes wishing is the wings the truth comes true on.

Sometimes the truth is what sets us wishing for it.

WORD

In Hebrew the term *dabar* means both "word" and "deed." Thus to say something is to do something. *I love you. I hate you. I forgive you. I am afraid.* Who knows what such words do, but whatever it is, it can never be undone. Something that lay hidden in the heart is irrevocably released through speech into time, is given substance and tossed like a stone into the pool of history, where the concentric rings lap out endlessly.

Words are power, essentially the power of creation. By my words I both discover and create who I am. By my words I elicit a word from you. Through our converse we create each other.

When God *said,* "Let there be light," there *was* light where before there was only darkness. When I *say* I love you, there *is* love where before there was only ambiguous silence. In a sense I do not love you first and then speak it, but only by speaking it give it reality.

"In the beginning was the Word," says John, meaning perhaps that before the beginning there was something like Silence: not the absence of sound, because there was no sound yet to be absent, but the absence of absence: nothing nothinged: everything. Then the Word. The Deed. The Beginning. The beginning in time of time. "The Word was with God, and the Word was God," says John. By uttering himself, God makes himself heard and makes himself hearers.

God never seems to weary of trying to get himself across. Word after word he tries in search of the right word. When the Creation itself doesn't seem to say it right—sun, moon, stars, all of it—he tries flesh and blood.

He tried saying it in Noah, but Noah was a drinking man. He tried saying it in Abraham, but Abraham was a little too Mesopotamian with all those wives and whiskers. He tried Moses, but Moses himself was trying too hard; tried David, but David was too pretty for his own good. Toward the end of his rope, God tried saying it in John the Baptist with his locusts and honey and hellfire preaching, and you get the feeling that John might almost have worked except that he lacked something small but crucial like a sense of the ridiculous or a balanced diet.

So he tried once more. Jesus as the *mot juste* of God.

"The word became flesh," John said, of all flesh *this* flesh. Jesus as the Word made flesh means take it or leave it: in this life, death, life, God finally manages to say what God is and what human is. It means: just as your words have you in them—your breath, spirit, power, hiddenness—so Jesus has God in him.

WORK (*See* VOCATION)

WORSHIP

Phrases like Worship Service or Service of Worship are tautologies. To worship God *means* to serve him. Basically there are two ways to do it. One way is to do things for him that he needs to have done—run errands for him, carry messages for him, fight on his side, feed his lambs, and so on. The other way is to do things for him that you need to do—sing songs for him, create beautiful things for him, give things up for him, tell him what's on your mind and in your heart, in general rejoice in him and make a fool of yourself for him the way lovers have always made fools of themselves for the one they love.

A Quaker Meeting, a Pontifical High Mass, the Family Service at First Presbyterian, a Holy Roller Happening—unless there is an element of joy and foolishness in the proceedings, the time would be better spent doing something useful.

Xx

X

X is the Greek letter *chi,* which is the first letter of the word Christ. Thus Xmas is shorthand for Christmas, taking only about one-sixth as long to write. If you do your cards by hand, it is possible to save as much as seventy-five or eighty minutes a year.

It is tempting to say that what you do with this time that you save is your own business. Briefly stated, however, the Christian position is that there's no such thing as your own business.

Yy

YHWH

In Exodus 3:13–14 when Moses asks God his name, God says his name is YHWH, which is apparently derived from the Hebrew verb *to be* and means something like "I am what I am" or "I will be what I will be." The original text of the Old Testament didn't include vowels, so YHWH is all that appears.

Since it was believed that God's name was too holy to be used by just anybody, over the years it came to be used only by the high priest on special occasions. When other people ran across it in their reading, they simply substituted for it the title Lord. The result of this pious practice was that in time no one knew any longer what vowels belonged in between the four consonants, and thus the proper pronunciation of God's name was lost. The best guess is that it was something like YaHWeH, but there's no way of being sure.

Like the bear in Thurber's fable, sometimes the pious lean so far over backward that they fall flat on their face.

Zz

ZACCHAEUS

The fact that his name begins with a *Z* is only one reason why Zacchaeus makes a good place to stop. He appears just once in the New Testament, and his story is brief (Luke 19:1–10). It is also one of the few places in the Gospels where we're given any visual detail. Maybe that is part of what makes it stand out.

We're told that Zacchaeus was a runt, for one thing. That is why when Jesus was reported to be en route into Jericho and the crowds gathered to see what they could see, Zacchaeus had to climb a tree to get a good look. Luke says the tree he climbed was a sycamore tree.

We're also told that Zacchaeus was a crook—a Jewish legman for the Roman IRS, who (following the practice of the day) raked in as much more than the going tax as he could get and pocketed the difference. When people saw Zacchaeus oiling down the street, they crossed to the other side.

The story goes like this. The sawed-off shyster is perched in the sycamore tree. Jesus opens his mouth to speak. All Jericho hugs itself in anticipation of hearing him give the man Holy Hell. *Woe unto you! Repent! Wise up!* is the least of what they expect. What Jesus says is, "Come down on the double. I'm staying at your house." The mob points out that the man Jesus is talking to is a public disaster. Jesus' silence is deafening.

It is not reported how Zacchaeus got out of the sycamore, but the chances are good that he fell out in pure astonishment.

He said, "I'm giving everything back. In spades." Maybe he even meant it. Jesus said, "Three cheers for the Irish!"

The unflagging lunacy of God. The unending seaminess of human beings. The meeting between them that is always a matter of life or death and usually both. The story of Zacchaeus is the Gospel in sycamore. It is the best and oldest joke in the world.